THE COOK BOOK OF LEFT-OVERS

A COLLECTION OF
400 RELIABLE RECIPES FOR
THE PRACTICAL HOUSEKEEPER

BY

HELEN CARROLL CLARKE
FORMER INSTRUCTOR IN COOKERY
IN PRATT INSTITUTE, BROOKLYN

AND

PHOEBE DEYO RULON
FORMER INSTRUCTOR IN INVALID
COOKERY AND DIETETICS IN BELLE-
VUE HOSPITAL, NEW YORK CITY

Creative Cookbooks
Monterey, California

The Cook Book of Left-Overs

by
Helen Carroll Clarke
Phoebe Deyo Rulon

ISBN: 1-58963-662-7

Copyright © 2002 by Fredonia Books

Reprinted from the 1911 edition

Creative Cookbooks
An Imprint of Fredonia Books
Monterey, California
http://www.creativecookbooks.com

All rights reserved, including the right to reproduce this book, or portions thereof, in any form.

In order to make original editions of historical works available to scholars at an economical price, this facsimile of the original edition of 1911 is reproduced from the best available copy and has been digitally enhanced to improve legibility, but the text remains unaltered to retain historical authenticity.

CONTENTS

	PAGE
Preface	vi
Introduction	3
Meats	5
What to do with Left-over Beef	7
What to do with Left-over Lamb and Mutton	23
What to do with Left-over Veal and Pork	33
What to do with Left-over Ham and Bacon	45
What to do with Left-over Poultry	53
Sauces	67
What to do with Left-over Fish	81
What to do with Left-over Vegetables	101
What to do with Left-over Cereals	131
What to do with Left-over Bread	149
What to do with Bits of Cheese	165
What to do with Sour Milk and Cream	177
What to do with Whites or Yolks of Eggs	187
What to do with Left-over Fruit	197
What to do with Left-over Beverages	213
What to do with Left-over Cake	223
Dainty Dishes from Little Bits	231
Index	235

PREFACE

This book is not intended as a substitute for the regular cook book. It aims to be simply a practical handybook for the average housekeeper, who cannot afford to waste food which has been left over from her table, and who nevertheless desires to serve the best and most attractive dishes.

In the average small family where there are no servants, or perhaps one servant, setting a table with the very least margin of ampleness means that there will inevitably follow some left-over food. In addition to this, it is sometimes wise deliberately to plan for a remainder (especially where the first-cooking process is a long one, or where the food itself admits of reheating to advantage) in order to spare time and labor to the cook. Therefore, both from necessity and choice, the interested home-maker finds herself facing the problem of how to make the most and best of a left-over food supply. It is for such women that this book has been written.

Many of the finest dishes—dishes over which

PREFACE

French chefs have made international reputations—are nothing more than "left-overs" attractively cooked. In every housekeeper's own kitchen there are the same foods, and the same possibilities.

And let it be added that in no branch of housekeeping or of cookery does a woman show to better advantage than in this ability to take the unrelated bits of left-over food and combine them so as to form tempting dishes for another meal.

THE COOK BOOK OF LEFT-OVERS

INTRODUCTION

What to Keep on Hand

From experience it has been found that it will facilitate the preparation of made-over dishes if the following supplies and utensils are always at hand:

Supplies

Seasonings, spices, and herbs of all kinds, including cayenne pepper or paprika.
Catsups and piquant sauces.
Small cans of vegetables, meats, fish, and soup.
Extract of beef or bouillon cubes.
Canned sweet peppers.
Salad dressings.
Tomato paste. (Italian stores carry this.)
Grated parmesan cheese, in bottles.
Jar of sifted bread-crumbs.
Unsweetened crackers.
Cans of sweetened condensed milk.
Cans of unsweetened evaporated milk.
Potato flour. (Jewish stores carry this.)

Utensils

Meat chopper.
Double boiler (or two saucepans that fit one in the other).

THE COOK BOOK OF LEFT-OVERS

Inexpensive wire frying-basket.
Individual baking-dishes, such as ramekins or shells.
Dover egg beater.

Measurements

All successful cooks measure. Some do it with their eyes, and with such nicety that they forget the process and declare they never measure, but to them a "lump" of butter and a "pinch" of seasoning are definite units of measurement. But these are unsafe guides to follow. For receipts in this book use the standard half-pint measuring-cup, with the subdivisions plainly marked.

All measures should be *level* for dry materials, and *full* for liquids. A "cup of milk" means a cup so filled that it cannot be safely carried across the room without spilling. Flour should be sifted once before measuring, and never packed down in the cup. A "spoonful" of dry ingredients, such as salt or flour, is not "heaping," but *level*—scraped level with a knife.

MEATS

Intelligent Buying of Meats

When buying meat remember the left-over which may follow, and which may need a sauce. Have all bones that are removed from roasts and other cuts of meat sent home from the market. They make excellent stock for sauces and soup. Always ask for a marrow-bone with all soup and stewing meat; marrow is an excellent shortening, and can be made into an acceptable luncheon dish. In preparing French chops, crown of lamb, and similar cuts for cooking, enough trimmings are often paid for and thrown away to make a savory dish. Have these sent home. Remember, an allowance of suet goes with most cuts of beef. Do not let it accumulate. Wipe carefully with a damp cloth, try out in a slow oven, and keep in a covered earthen jar. Keep all fat from fried bacon in a separate jar; it is valuable for browning and seasoning purposes. Equal parts of chicken fat, flank suet, and butter make an excellent shortening, which will keep for some time in a cool place, and can be used instead of butter.

THE COOK BOOK OF LEFT-OVERS

Intelligent Cooking of Left-over Meats

The greatest care must be taken not to destroy their digestibility. Never subject them to great heat for a long time. Whenever possible, let a hot sauce do most of the heating of rare, tender meat. Long, slow cooking is sometimes necessary to blend flavors and soften the hardened fibers of some cooked meats, but always keep the heat moderate. A double boiler is a good utensil for such cooking.

Intelligent Seasoning of Left-over Meats

As a rule, reheated meats need to be more highly seasoned than freshly cooked ones. It is not wise, however, to crowd too many flavors into one dish, or always use the same seasoning for the same dish. The exact amount of salt and pepper must be determined by the seasoning already in the meat.

Intelligent Care of Left-over Meat

Eternal vigilance is the price of health. Cooked meats are particularly attractive to flies, and flies are deadly. Do not put warm meat in the ice-box. Cover while cooling with inexpensive wire covers that come for the purpose. Do not forget it after it goes in the ice-box, but arrange for its prompt use.

WHAT TO DO WITH LEFT-OVER BEEF

The Sunday Roast and Good Carving
Practise the art of good carving. A well-carved joint looks better, tastes better, and goes further.

Cold Roast Beef with Horseradish Sauce
Let the first use of left-over roast beef be the serving of it sliced and cold—it is a mistake to miss this use. Cut thin slices of the rare beef, arrange nicely on a cold platter, and garnish with something green and crisp. Vary by serving different cold sauces with the meat. Serve a vegetable salad at the same meal.

Horseradish Sauce
Season two tablespoonfuls of grated horseradish with one-quarter teaspoonful each of salt and sugar, and one tablespoonful of vinegar. Whip one-quarter cup of thick cream stiff and add it to the horseradish. If there is no cream, a good sauce may be made by soaking an equal quantity of grated horseradish and soft white bread-crumbs with twice as much milk, until the mass is quite

soft. Season with salt, sugar, and vinegar, and press through a fine wire sieve. The sauce should be of creamy thickness.

Roast Beef Sandwiches, Served Hot

For four good-sized sandwiches make one cup of brown sauce (see page 68), adding to it. when cooked, one tablespoonful of finely minced sour pickle. Cut very thin as many slices of cold rare roast beef as needed. Cream two tablespoonfuls of butter and add to it one-quarter teaspoonful of made mustard. Spread the bread with this. Dip the slices of beef in the hot sauce and place them on the bread. Sprinkle with a very little chopped or crushed cold bacon before putting on the top slice of bread. Serve on a hot platter and pour the boiling sauce over all.

Rare Roast Beef in Savory Tomato Sauce

Boil together for ten minutes

2 cups tomatoes	Bit of bay leaf
2 cloves	Sprig of parsley
3 peppercorns	½ teaspoonful salt

Strain. Melt two tablespoonfuls butter; when bubbling, add two tablespoonfuls flour and stir until blended. Gradually add the tomato, beating to avoid thickening unevenly. Let sauce boil up for one minute. Arrange the beef on a *hot* platter and pour the boiling sauce over it. One teaspoonful of chopped parsley may be added to the sauce just before taking up.

BEEF

Beef Loaf (of Cold Beef)

This is an acceptable way of using any of the small pieces of "well-done" roast beef, making an excellent luncheon or supper dish, especially in hot weather.

Soak one tablespoonful of gelatine in one-half cup of cold water ten minutes. Heat three-quarters of a cup of well-seasoned stewed tomatoes to boiling, and pour over the gelatine, stirring well until gelatine is dissolved. Have ready two cups of chopped and seasoned meat, mixed with one tablespoonful of lemon-juice and one small sour pickle minced fine. Stir the tomato into the meat mixture, and mold in an earthen dish. This amount will fill a quart dish half full.

Beef Pie

Cut cold roast beef into inch-square pieces, using two cups. Put into a quart baking-dish and season with one-half teaspoonful of salt, a little pepper, one tablespoonful of tomato catsup or one-third cup of cooked and seasoned tomatoes. Pour over the meat one cup of liquid, using equal quantities of made gravy and hot water. Cover with a crust made of baking-powder-biscuit dough. For this amount of meat use for the dough

½ cup flour
1 tablespoonful butter
1 teaspoonful baking-powder
¼ teaspoonful salt
About ¼ cup of milk

Fire Island Stew

A good Monday dinner when a Sunday roast and macaroni have preceded it.

Melt two tablespoonfuls of butter, add one small sliced onion, and cook together until very slightly browned. To this add one and one-half cups of stewed tomatoes and let boil slowly for about fifteen minutes, or until the tomato is somewhat thickened. Then add one and one-half cups of cooked macaroni and let all cook together until well thickened. Just before the dinner hour, put into the saucepan one and one-half to two cups of remnants of the tender roast beef, cut small, and let heat. A very few minutes will suffice. Do not let the stew boil after the meat is added.

Beef Soufflé

2 cups chopped beef
1 cup fresh bread-crumbs
2 cups white sauce No. 2 (page 68)
2 eggs
1 teaspoonful of chopped parsley
1 teaspoonful onion-juice

Have the white sauce ready and cooled. Season the meat with salt, pepper, chopped parsley, and onion-juice. Mix meat, bread-crumbs, and white sauce well together. Separate the eggs and add the beaten yolks to the meat mixture. Beat the whites stiff and carefully fold them in. Turn the mixture into a well-buttered baking-dish and bake in a hot oven fifteen minutes. Serve at once in the dish in which it is baked.

Pot-Roast Pie

Remove the seeds and parboil one medium-sized sweet green pepper in boiling water for five minutes. Cut into thin slices and sprinkle a few in the bot-

BEEF

tom of an earthen baking-dish. Cover with thin slices of cold pot-roast. Add a few fine bread-crumbs, moisten with any of the pot-roast gravy at hand, or stock. Repeat until the dish is nearly filled.

Peel four good-sized tomatoes, if in season; cut in halves and place on top. Or the whole ones from a can may be used instead. Season thoroughly with salt and pepper and finish with a sprinkling of well-buttered crumbs. Bake in a moderate oven until the tomatoes are tender, covering for the first ten minutes. Serve in the baking-dish.

Braised Meat Balls (from Meat Trimmings)

2 cups meat
1 teaspoonful salt
¼ teaspoonful pepper
2 tablespoonfuls fine bread-crumbs
1 egg

Carefully wipe, and remove most of the fat from, any tough ends of uncooked beefsteak, or other meat trimmings of beef or lamb, or both. Put them through a meat chopper or chop fine. Mix all together and form into balls—this amount will make eight medium-sized ones. Brown lightly in a little bacon fat. Put one-half can of well-seasoned tomatoes in an earthen baking-dish or casserole. Add one cup each of carrots and celery cut in cubes, one slice of green pepper, one teaspoonful of salt, and one-quarter teaspoonful of pepper. Lay the meat balls on top, add any bacon fat left from browning them, and cover the dish tightly. Cook slowly in a moderate oven until the vegetables are tender—about two hours. Serve in the baking-dish.

THE COOK BOOK OF LEFT-OVERS

Twentieth-Century Hash

Have baked six medium-sized potatoes. With a spoon carefully remove the potato, leaving rest of skin unbroken. Season the potato with one tablespoonful of butter, one tablespoonful of cream or milk, one teaspoonful of salt, and a little pepper, stirring lightly with a fork, but do not mash the potato. Add one cup of any kind of well-seasoned chopped beef that has been moistened with a little gravy, stock, or Worcestershire sauce. Fill the skins with this mixture, letting it rise a little above the top. Put a piece of butter on each and heat in oven. Grated cheese may be used instead of meat.

Surprise Biscuits (with Beef)

1½ cups flour	3 teaspoonfuls baking-powder
2 tablespoonfuls shortening	½ teaspoonful salt
About ½ cup of milk	

Make a biscuit dough as soft as can be handled, pat it lightly, roll into a thin sheet, and cut with a biscuit cutter. Have ready one cup of well-seasoned minced beef that has been moistened with a little gravy, stock, or milk. Form into sandwiches by spreading the meat lightly on half of the biscuits and cover with the other half, pressing them together at the edges. Bake twenty minutes in a hot oven. This amount will make nine good-sized sandwiches. A brown gravy may be poured over them if desired. Serve hot.

Stuffed Peppers (with Beef)

Parboil four to six green peppers for five minutes. Prepare a mixture of cooked rice and rare

BEEF

roast beef or steak, seasoned and chopped fine. Moisten with a little brown sauce (see page 68) made from soup stock. Stuff the peppers with this mixture and put buttered bread-crumbs on top. Place in a baking-pan and bake about twenty minutes in a moderate oven, basting with water and butter—one tablespoonful of butter to half a cup of hot water—as they cook. Serve on small pieces of toast and pour the remaining brown sauce around.

Stuffed Cabbage (with Beef) with Brown Sauce

Use Savoy cabbage. Wash it and put in boiling water for five minutes to allow the leaves to open. Chop and season the remnants of rare roast beef and put the meat between the leaves of the cabbage. Tie the cabbage carefully to retain the shape. Have ready two cups of brown sauce (see page 68) and add to it two tablespoonfuls of vinegar and a few slices of carrot and onion. Put the cabbage in the sauce, and cook very slowly about three hours. Baste occasionally.

Minced Beef with Potato Border

To two cups of well-seasoned mashed potato add the yolks of two eggs. Beat together until very light and creamy. Form this mixture into a border on a round, flat baking-dish. Score the top. Season two cups of any kind of cold chopped beef with one-half teaspoonful of onion-juice, obtained by pressing the cut surface of an onion against a grater and moving it slightly; one teaspoonful finely chopped parsley, salt and pepper. Add enough stock or milk to moisten it well. Place the

THE COOK BOOK OF LEFT-OVERS

meat inside of the potato border and brown lightly in a hot oven.

A Scallop of Roast Beef with Rice

Season the rice with one teaspoonful of bacon fat to each cup of cooked rice used, and put a layer in a baking-dish. Cover with cold roast beef chopped not too fine, then a layer of sliced or stewed tomatoes, seasoned well with salt, pepper, and dots of butter. Repeat until the dish is nearly filled, and cover with buttered bread-crumbs. Brown lightly in oven. If sliced tomatoes are used, cook until these are tender.

Irish Rissoles

Any kind of meat may be used for these, preferably rare roast beef or steak. Put the meat through the meat grinder together with enough chives to flavor it. (A little onion may be used if chives cannot be obtained.) Add soft bread-crumbs from inside of loaf, seasoning, and enough milk to shape the rissoles. Form into round balls and sauté in a very little hot fat, turning them often, that all sides may be brown. For five small rissoles use one cup of minced beef, a few chives, or half a small onion, nearly a cup of bread-crumbs, and a third of a cup of milk. They may be served plain or with white sauce, and are very quickly made.

Meat Dumplings

Season one cup of chopped meat with salt, pepper, and a drop or two of Tabasco sauce. Sift together three-quarters of a cup of flour, one and

BEEF

one-half teaspoonfuls of baking-powder, and one-eighth teaspoonful of salt. Beat one egg until light, add to it two tablespoonfuls of milk, and stir this into the flour mixture. If this does not wet up all of the flour add more milk. The dough should be very stiff. Stir the meat into this, and drop by spoonfuls into boiling stock or boiling salted water and cook, tightly covered, about ten minutes. Serve at once with tomato sauce.

Shepherd's Pie

Minced roast beef
Mashed potatoes
Salt and pepper
Butter (mashed with potatoes)
Roast beef gravy

Put beef and potatoes in layers in a buttered baking-dish, having potatoes at the bottom. Moisten meat layers generously with gravy. Season to taste. Have top layer potatoes; dot over with bits of butter, and brown. This dish requires much rich gravy.

Roast Lamb or Beef Re-heated

In warming up a leg of lamb or standing rib-roast of beef heap up the cavity left after carving with mashed potato. Brush over with melted butter and brown in oven.

Beef Balls with Horseradish Sauce

Season a cup and a half of cold chopped beef with salt, pepper, celery salt, very little onion-juice, and lemon-juice; add one beaten egg and form into balls. Roll the balls in a very little butter in a frying-pan, and toss the balls around

THE COOK BOOK OF LEFT-OVERS

in it until well heated. Serve with horseradish sauce (see page 7).

Corned-Beef Hash

This dish is most acceptably prepared by using some of the fat meat chopped with the lean. To two cups of meat chopped rather coarse, allow two cups of chopped potatoes. If the meat is all lean, pour two tablespoonfuls of melted butter over the potatoes before mixing them with the beef. Moisten well with milk or stock, using at least one-half cup of liquid. Season with salt and pepper. Melt a little butter in a frying-pan, put in the hash, cover tightly, and cook slowly on the cool part of the stove for at least half an hour. It should be brown and crusty on the bottom. If it is not, increase the heat just before turning out.

Corned-Beef-and-Beet Hash

Use about equal amounts of cooked corned beef and boiled potatoes, and a little less quantity of cooked beets. Chop all three separately. Mix and season with salt and pepper. Try out a few thin slices of fat salt pork until crisp, chop and add to mixture; use the fat (or part of it) in warming up the hash. Moisten with hot water. Heat in hot frying-pan, turning often to keep it from sticking. This mixture may be formed into balls, rolled in flour, and then browned.

Corned Beef Creamed

Slice any remnants of cold corned beef in thin pieces to make two cups. Make two cups white sauce No. 2 (see page 68). Cook until smooth

BEEF

and thickened, then add the two cups of beef. Cook very slowly together for fifteen minutes.

Beef Soup

A good soup can be made of the bones and "odds and ends" of the roast, with the usual vegetables and seasonings, but the soup will be better if a little fresh soup meat, or perhaps end pieces from the steak or new roast, be used as well. Put all the meat into a soup-kettle together with a sliced onion, carrot, and a small portion of Russia turnip, some stalks of celery, two or three sprigs of parsley, six cloves, six peppercorns, a bay leaf, and one teaspoonful of salt. Barely cover with cold water and allow it to stand awhile before putting on the stove. Let cook slowly for four or five hours. Strain and set aside in a cold place for use next day. Remove the fat, season to taste, and serve clear, or with diced vegetables which have been first cooked in water and added to the soup ten minutes before serving. Do not serve this soup the same day in which it is cooked, for it will have a greasy appearance and taste.

Deviled Marrow on Crackers

When the marrow is not wanted in the soup, it can be served on crisp crackers for lunch, and makes a nutritious dish. Scrape the marrow-bones, wash them well, and cover top and bottom with paste made of flour and water. Tie in clean cheesecloth, and boil for three-quarters of an hour. Remove cloth and paste, and take marrow out from bones. Season highly with paprika. Serve on crisp crackers.

Beef Croquettes Made from Soup Meat

Chop the meat very fine. Season highly with salt, pepper, and celery salt. Add a little grated nutmeg if desired. To two cups of the chopped meat add one beaten egg, and moisten with enough thick tomato sauce (see page 71) to shape into croquettes. Roll in egg and crumbs, and fry in deep fat. Serve with the remainder of the tomato sauce re-heated and thinned.

Savory Meat

Soup meat, 1 lb.
Stock, 1 cup
Celery salt, 1 teaspoonful
Summer savory, ¼ teaspoonful
Sweet marjoram, ¼ teaspoonful
Grated onion, ½ teaspoonful
Salt, ½ teaspoonful
White pepper, ¼ teaspoonful
Nutmeg
Paprika

Chop the meat fine, removing all gristle. Season, moisten with the stock, and press into a small bread-pan. Put into the oven for a few minutes. When cold, slice.

By the long process of soup-making, flavor has been taken from the meat, but it still has food value. It should be highly seasoned to make it palatable.

Beef Scallop

See Lamb Scallop, p. 26.

MY OWN RECEIPTS

MY OWN RECEIPTS

MY OWN RECEIPTS

MY OWN RECEIPTS

WHAT TO DO WITH LEFT-OVER LAMB AND MUTTON

Sliced Lamb with Olive Sauce

Have ready two dozen medium-sized olives that have been cooked in boiling water thirty minutes and then stoned.

2 tablespoonfuls of minced onion	$\frac{1}{2}$ teaspoonfuls of salt
4 tablespoonfuls of butter	$\frac{1}{8}$ teaspoonful of pepper
	2 cups hot stock
4 tablespoonfuls of flour	

Brown the onion lightly in the butter, add the flour and seasonings, and cook until bubbling, then add two cups of stock—made from the bones of the roast and odds and ends of meat—and cook and stir until thick and smooth. Then add the olives. Season thin slices of cold roast lamb with salt and pepper, and add to the sauce. Simmer gently five minutes. When ready to serve, add one tablespoonful of lemon-juice. Pour on a hot platter and garnish with hominy balls (see page 133).

Lamb, Turkish Style

Brown a small onion and one-third cup of well-washed rice in butter or beef drippings. Add one cup of stewed tomatoes, one cup of lamb or mutton cut in squares, four tablespoonfuls of minced carrot, one teaspoonful of horseradish, salt and pepper to taste. Make quite moist with gravy or hot water. Cover closely and simmer until the rice is soft and the water absorbed. If the mixture should become too dry, add more wetting. Serve on a hot platter and garnish with triangles of nicely browned toast. This dish in Turkey is called *Pilau*.

Lamb in Ambush

Mince the lamb very fine. To each cup of meat allow one teaspoonful of chopped capers, one-half teaspoonful of onion-juice, one-quarter teaspoonful of salt, and a little paprika. Moisten with four tablespoonfuls of gravy or stock. Butter a deep pan or mold. Line the bottom and sides one inch deep with warm, well-seasoned mashed potato. Fill the center with the meat mixture, and spread potato over the top. Cover tightly and steam, or set in pan of water and cook in oven from one-half to three-quarters of an hour. Turn out carefully on a hot platter, and serve tomato sauce (see page 71) in a separate dish. This dish is often called *Lamb Chartreuse*.

Oriental Stew

Simmer gently together

2 cups of cold lamb or mutton cut in cubes	1 chopped onion
	2 small cold potatoes, sliced
1 cup of water	1 cup of cooked peas or cooked string beans chopped
2 tablespoonfuls of butter	

LAMB AND MUTTON

Season with salt, pepper, and a very little curry powder, if liked. While the stew is heating, boil one-half cup of well-washed rice. When tender, put into a hot vegetable dish, hollow the center, and turn in the stew. Serve at once.

Spanish Stew

Melt two tablespoonfuls of butter, slice two small onions, and mix with two cups of chopped meat, not fine. The meat may be all lamb or a mixture of lamb and beef. Brown all together in the butter. Add one teaspoonful of flour, four medium-sized tomatoes, one tablespoonful Chili sauce, one seeded red pepper, cut fine, one tablespoonful salt, and two cups of stock. Cover and let simmer until well blended and thickened. Serve on a platter and garnish with radishes and parsley.

Old Homestead Pie

Cut the remnants of any cold boiled mutton into very thin slices, seasoning each slice with salt, pepper, and a little paprika. Arrange them in layers in a suitable baking-dish. Heat any leftover caper sauce, and if necessary add enough fresh sauce to well cover each layer of meat. Have ready two cups of well-seasoned, hot mashed potato and turnip, using one and one-half cups of mashed potato to one-half cup of mashed turnip. Be careful to have them well seasoned and well beaten, and then press through a ricer (or coarse sieve), letting the mixture fall lightly over the top of the pie as a cover. Brush the top with egg yolk beaten lightly with a little water. Brown lightly in the oven. Serve currant jelly with this dish.

Mutton or Lamb Croquettes

2 cups finely chopped meat
1 tablespoonful chopped capers
1 cup cooked rice
1 tablespoonful lemon-juice
Salt and paprika
1 cup white sauce No. 2 (see page 68)

Mix all together and set away to get cold. When ready to form, take up by full tablespoonfuls and shape into cylinders. Roll gently in finely sifted white bread-crumbs, then in egg (slightly beaten with one tablespoonful of cold water), being careful that *every* part of the croquette is covered with egg, and then again in crumbs. Put in a frying-basket and brown lightly in smoking-hot fat. They will brown very quickly.

Lamb Scallop

Stale bread-crumbs
A bit of onion
Gravy thinned with hot water
Salt and pepper
½ cup fresh or stewed tomato, or a little lemon-juice
Butter
Meat cut in small pieces

Into a buttered baking-dish, holding about a quart, put a layer of bread-crumbs, then a layer of meat, seasoning and adding a little grated onion. Repeat until the dish is nearly full. Add tomatoes, or a tablespoonful of tomato catsup, or a little lemon-juice. Cover with a layer of crumbs. Pour the gravy, thinned with hot water, into the dish until it can just be seen. Put bits of butter over the top, and bake in a moderate oven from one-half to three-quarters of an hour. Increase

LAMB AND MUTTON

the heat to brown the crumbs on top, and serve hot. Beef or veal may be used instead of lamb.

Lamb's Liver Hash

Chop fine some left-over liver and heart which have been steamed or sautéd. Add nearly twice as much seasoned left-over or fresh mashed potatoes. Moisten well with stock or gravy, add more seasoning, put into pan with hot bacon fat, and sauté slowly until a brown crust has formed underneath. Fold hash over in pan, turn out on platter, and dress with plenty of fresh parsley. Lamb's liver is excellent and inexpensive, and should be more generally used.

Patty-Pan Pies

Cut any remnants of baked or boiled lamb or mutton in small pieces, discarding all bone and gristle. Season with salt, pepper, and a little onion-juice if desired. For two cups of such meat allow one cup of any left-over gravy diluted with a little hot water, or one cup of good stock made from the bones and bits of meat, flavored with vegetables, and thickened with one tablespoonful of flour. Heat meat and gravy together. Line patty-pans with good plain pastry, rolled rather thin. Fill with the warm meat and cover with pastry. Bake in rather a moderate oven until the pastry is cooked, about half an hour. Each patty makes an individual portion, and can be served with or without brown sauce (see page 68).

Plain Pastry for Four Patty Pies

Sift together one and one-half cups of pastry flour, one-half teaspoonful each of salt and baking-powder. Into this chop four tablespoonfuls of any shortening desired, and add slowly enough ice-water to moisten, about six tablespoonfuls. The dough should be very stiff. Roll out and spread the surface with two tablespoonfuls of butter, fold over and roll again. It is well to let it stand in a cold place some time before using. Wrapped in a napkin it will keep several days in the ice-box.

Panned Lamb (with Oysters)

1½ cups lamb, chopped fine
6 oysters
2 tablespoonfuls butter
Salt and pepper
Gravy or stock

Heat oysters with butter. When they curl add meat and seasoning. Moisten with gravy or stock. Cover and simmer ten minutes. Serve on hot toast.

MY OWN RECEIPTS

MY OWN RECEIPTS

MY OWN RECEIPTS

MY OWN RECEIPTS

WHAT TO DO WITH LEFT-OVER VEAL AND PORK

Blanket of Veal

This dish may be prepared, if desired, from a mixture of cooked and uncooked veal. Discard all gristle and hard portions of any roasted veal. Cut in inch squares. To one cup of such meat allow three-quarters of a pound of uncooked breast of veal. Cover the raw meat with hot—not boiling —water. Add any bones from the roast, and two tablespoonfuls of any flavoring vegetables at hand (such as carrots, celery, and turnips, chopped), a sprig of parsley, one bay leaf, one teaspoonful of salt, and one-quarter teaspoonful of pepper. Cover and cook slowly until veal is nearly tender, then add the cold meat, and simmer gently ten minutes longer. Take out the meat and strain the broth. There should be two cups; if not, make up with boiling water. Melt two tablespoonfuls of butter, stir in two tablespoonfuls of flour, and add the hot broth. When thickened, add one egg yolk beaten up with four tablespoonfuls of cream or rich milk. Remove from the fire at once, add one tablespoonful of lemon-juice, and pour over the hot meat.

One cup of cooked peas may be added to the sauce if desired. This dish is often called *Veau à la Blanquette*.

Veal Scallop with Oysters

To every cup of finely chopped veal allow twelve good-sized oysters. Season the meat highly with salt, paprika, and one teaspoonful of lemon-juice. Moisten it with a little stock. Arrange in layers in a baking-dish beginning with the veal, and sprinkle some well-buttered cracker-crumbs between each layer and on top. Add one-half cup thin cream or milk, and one-half cup of strained oyster liquor, to each measure of veal. Bake in a hot oven about fifteen minutes.

Jellied Veal

When ordering a roast of veal have some bones sent home with it. Wash these well, cover with cold water, add one cup of diced vegetables—carrot, turnip, celery, onion, and one bay leaf—and let simmer for three or four hours. Strain the stock, let it cool, cover, and set in the ice-box. This will keep for several days. When ready to use skim off any fat on top, and to each cup of stock add one-quarter teaspoonful of salt, one-eighth teaspoonful of pepper, one-half teaspoonful of lemon-juice, and a very little paprika. Cut any remaining veal in thin slivers—there should be an equal quantity of meat and stock—and simmer together until the veal is moist and tender. If the meat falls short, use two or three " hard-boiled " eggs cut in neat slices and mixed with the meat after it is removed from the fire. Mold in a bread-pan and serve cold.

VEAL AND PORK

Creamed Veal on Hot Biscuits

Season two cups of chopped veal with one teaspoonful of finely chopped capers, one teaspoonful of lemon-juice, salt, pepper, and a slight grating of nutmeg, if desired. Melt one tablespoonful of butter, stir in one-half tablespoonful of flour, one-quarter teaspoonful of salt, and add slowly one-half cup of cream or rich milk, and cook until sauce thickens. Mix one egg yolk with one teaspoonful cold water and add to sauce, together with the seasoned veal. Remove from the fire as soon as meat is heated, and serve on hot biscuits.

Veal and Potato Puff

Season two cups of finely chopped veal with salt, paprika, and one tablespoonful catsup. Moisten with a little gravy or stock. Have ready two cups of well-seasoned mashed potato, add to them the yolks of two eggs, and beat until very light and creamy. Fold in the stiffly beaten whites of the two eggs. Butter a baking-dish, and cover the bottom with half of the potato, spread all of the meat on top, and cover with the rest of the potato. Brown in hot oven.

Veal in Batter

1 egg
4 tablespoonfuls milk
½ tablespoonful olive or any good salad oil
½ tablespoonful lemon-juice
Scant ½ cup sifted flour
1¾ cups chopped veal
¼ teaspoonful salt
A little white pepper

To the well-beaten yolk of the egg add the milk, oil, seasoning, flour, and lemon-juice. Beat the white of the egg stiff, and add to batter when ready to use. Stir into this the veal, which should not be chopped fine. Drop by spoonfuls into slightly smoking fat, and fry slowly to a golden brown. Drain on soft paper or cheese-cloth. These fritters may be served with or without a sauce. Chicken may be used instead of veal.

Veal Rolls

Cut the veal in slices, spread each one with the stuffing left from the roast, or with bread-crumbs seasoned and moistened with butter, roll up tightly and tie. Roll with flour, sprinkle with salt and pepper, brown slowly in hot butter, then half cover with rich milk or veal stock in which one teaspoonful of flour has been blended, simmer ten minutes. Remove the strings and serve on hot toast.

Croquettes (with Stock)

2 cups beef, veal, chicken, or lobster	1 cup stock
	2 teaspoonfuls lemon-juice
2 tablespoonfuls butter	Salt and pepper
4 tablespoonfuls flour	Dash of cayenne

Cook flour in hot butter, add stock gradually, and boil up well. Season meat highly with salt, pepper, cayenne, and lemon-juice, and put into stock. When almost to boiling-point, remove from fire and set aside to cool. Shape into balls. If too soft to handle add fine-sifted bread-crumbs; do not add flour for stiffening croquettes. Roll in crumbs, in egg, in crumbs again, and fry in smoking-hot fat two minutes.

VEAL AND PORK

Veal Loaf

1 lb. lean cold roast veal	1 teaspoonful salt
⅛ lb. cooked chopped bacon	¼ teaspoonful mace
2 pounded crackers	¼ teaspoonful pepper
1 well-beaten egg	Gravy
	Dash of cayenne

Put the meat through a meat grinder, add the other ingredients, moisten with left-over gravy, and season more highly if necessary. Grease a shallow pan with bacon fat, put in loaf, and press into shape, adding a little more thin gravy. Bake half an hour, or until brown on top.

Quick Veal-and-Sago Soup

1 lb. lean veal, chopped	Soup celery and parsley
1 carrot cut in pieces	2 tablespoonfuls sago
1 small onion	1½ cups scalded milk
1 egg	Salt and pepper

Cover veal with cold water, add carrot, onion, celery, parsley, salt, and pepper. Heat gradually and boil one hour. Strain. Soak sago in water half an hour, strain, add to soup, and cook until sago is clear. Add milk and more seasoning if necessary. Beat egg, place in tureen, pour soup over it, stirring well.

Veal on Toast

Cut cold roast veal into small pieces. Prepare slices of crisp, dried toast and place on a platter in the oven. Take some of yesterday's left-over veal gravy, thin it with an equal quantity of hot water, and pour into a frying-pan. Let the gravy boil. Just before serving add the cold veal; heat thoroughly, but do not boil. Place meat on the toast, pour gravy around it, and garnish dish with thin slices of lemon.

Veal with Clams

2 cups chopped veal
1 cup chopped clams
Salt and pepper
1 tablespoonful butter
4 tablespoonfuls clam-juice
½ cup well-seasoned mashed potato

Mix veal, clams, and juice, then season. Put mixture in buttered ramekins. Cover with mashed potato. Dot with bits of butter. Bake fifteen minutes in hot oven.

Veal Scallop

See Lamb Scallop, p. 26.

Savory Fresh Pork

2 cups chopped meat
2 tablespoonfuls butter
1 cup cooked tomatoes
2 tablespoonfuls of flour
1 small onion
1 cup of gravy or meat stock

Salt, and red pepper, small, and chopped very fine

Slice the onion and brown it delicately in the butter. Then add the flour and stir until well blended. Turn in the tomatoes, gravy, and meat. Add the seasoning and cook until well heated. Serve on a hot platter with baked potatoes.

Fresh Pork with Baked Apples

Mince any remnants of roast pork to make two cupfuls. Season it as needed with salt and a little

VEAL AND PORK

pepper and moisten with a few spoonfuls of gravy. Wash half a dozen medium-sized greening apples. Cut a slice from the stem end, take out all of the core and enough of the apple part to form a neat cup. Put the meat in these, with a small piece of butter on top of each. Place them in an agate baking-pan, add a very little water, and bake until the apples are soft.

Pork with Fried Apples

Cut cold roast pork into small pieces. Thin the left-over gravy with a little hot water, adding seasoning, if necessary. Let it boil for a few minutes in a frying-pan. Add the meat, heat thoroughly, but do not allow the sauce to boil. Serve with apples prepared as follows: Core three or four Baldwin apples without removing the skin. Cut into slices half an inch thick, and cook in hot bacon fat until soft and well browned. Drain on soft paper. Or the pork may be sliced and served cold, and the apples used as a border.

A Scallop of Roast Pork and Cabbage

2 cups thinly slivered pork
$1\frac{1}{2}$ cups cooked chopped cabbage
$1\frac{1}{2}$ cups white sauce No. 2 (see page 68)

Season pork with salt and pepper. In a baking-dish arrange layers of pork, cabbage, and white sauce. Cover with a few well-buttered crumbs. Heat in oven until sauce bubbles through the crumbs.

Mock Chicken Salad

Cut any cold fresh pork in pieces suitable for salad. To two cups of such meat add three tablespoonfuls of hot vinegar and set away to get very cold. When ready to prepare the salad, drain off any of the vinegar remaining and add one and one-half cups of crisp celery cut small, and pour over all a cooked salad dressing (see page 75). Serve on crisp lettuce leaves.

> # MY OWN RECEIPTS

MY OWN RECEIPTS

MY OWN RECEIPTS

MY OWN RECEIPTS

WHAT TO DO WITH LEFT-OVER HAM AND BACON

Baked Ham and Eggs

Butter a shallow baking-dish and sprinkle two tablespoonfuls of well-buttered soft bread-crumbs on the bottom. Add one cup of cooked ham chopped and one-quarter cup of hot milk. Break on top the number of eggs desired. Season and sprinkle with a few fine white crumbs, well buttered. Bake until the eggs are sufficiently cooked. Garnish with a little finely chopped water-cress, if at hand, and serve in the baking-dish.

Ham with Macaroni

Boil a scant three-quarters cup of broken macaroni in plenty of boiling, salted water until tender—about forty minutes. This should make two cups when cooked. Drain and rinse well under cold water so it will not be pasty. Add four tablespoonfuls of grated cheese. Reheat over hot water, adding enough cream or milk to moisten—about one tablespoonful. When well heated mix in lightly with a fork one cup chopped cooked ham that has been moistened with four tablespoonfuls

THE COOK BOOK OF LEFT-OVERS

of mustard sauce (see page 75). This makes a good luncheon dish, and can be prepared with two cups of any cold macaroni and cheese.

Ham Omelet

Make white sauce No. 1 A (see page 68), and cool slightly. Chop enough cold ham to make four full tablespoonfuls. Beat the whites of four eggs stiff. Beat the yolks until thick, then add salt and pepper and four tablespoonfuls of the white sauce. Cut and fold into this mixture the beaten whites of the eggs.

Melt a tablespoonful of butter in a frying-pan, pour the omelet into this, and cook over a slow fire until it has puffed up and is slightly browned underneath. Sprinkle the ham over the surface and place in the oven a moment to "set" the top of the omelet. Do not leave it, or it will become too dry. Fold over, turn out on a hot platter, and serve immediately with the remainder of the white sauce poured around it. Parsley may be added, either as a garnish or chopped and mixed with the white sauce.

Creamed Ham (in Chafing-dish)

Remove yolks from three or four hard-cooked eggs, and cut the whites in rings. Have ready minced seasoned ham, prepared by chopping fine or putting through meat grinder any small left-over pieces. Make in the chafing-dish white sauce No. 2, put ham in, and heat through. (Do not let boil while making these additions.) Add whites of eggs, season highly, grate yolks over top, and serve from dish.

HAM AND BACON

Ham Cakes

Mix a few spoonfuls of cooked ham chopped fine with two cups well-seasoned mashed potatoes. Brown in a little hot bacon fat.

Ham Sandwich Filling

Chop very fine the meat from the shank of boiled ham. Mix with enough boiled salad dressing (see page 75) to make thick paste. Pack in glass jar. This will keep in a cold place for a long time.

Poached Egg on Yankee Toast

While the eggs are poaching, carefully brown some neatly trimmed slices of bread in a little bacon fat. Crush a slice of cold, crisp bacon, and sprinkle a very little on each slice of toast, and serve the egg on top. Shred a leaf or two of crisp lettuce *very* fine and garnish the top of each egg.

Liver-and-Bacon Hash

Chop any cold cooked liver, and season with salt and pepper. Crush a few slices of cold, crisp bacon and add to it. To every cup of liver allow four tablespoonfuls of cooked rice, or any coarse cereal, and mix lightly together. Melt two tablespoonfuls of butter or drippings in a frying-pan, add one-quarter cup of tomatoes, and turn in the meat mixture. Cover and simmer slowly until well heated. Serve on a hot platter, and garnish with nicely browned potato cakes.

Minced Liver

To each cup of cold, minced liver, add one tablespoonful of chopped onion browned in butter, and season with salt and a little paprika. Turn into an agate frying-pan with a little water. Sprinkle lightly with flour and add one-quarter cup of vinegar. Simmer until well heated.

Sausage-and-Rice Cakes

To one cup of cooked rice—warm or cold—add one egg unbeaten and two tablespoonfuls of cold fried sausage. Mix well together and form into flat cakes. If the mixture is very soft, add a little more rice. Brown lightly in butter or drippings, being careful to have the fat well heated before adding the cakes. This amount will make six medium-sized ones.

MY OWN RECEIPTS

MY OWN RECEIPTS

MY OWN RECEIPTS

MY OWN RECEIPTS

WHAT TO DO WITH LEFT-OVER POULTRY

Chicken Salad

Cut the cold chicken from the bones, using all the small bits. Have pieces uniform in size, and in shape of small cubes. Scrape celery and let stand several hours in ice-water, then dry in a clean napkin. Use half as much celery as chicken, and cut into pieces half the size. Make a French dressing of

| 1 tablespoonful lemon-juice | ¼ teaspoonful salt |
| 3 tablespoonfuls oil | ⅛ teaspoonful white pepper |

Pour this over the chicken and celery, mix well, and put into ice-box to stand for fifteen minutes. Drain the liquid from some canned sweet red peppers, and chop with stoned olives. Mix with the salad, and just before it is served pour mayonnaise dressing over it (see page 74), tossing it over and over with a silver fork until each piece is coated with the dressing. Put into a salad bowl, or on individual plates, and garnish with small tender ends and leaves of the celery, whole olives, and a few tiny cucumber pickles. Serve very cold.

Creamed Chicken

Make a white sauce No. 2 (see page 68). When hot put into it small pieces of chicken, and half as much diced cooked sweetbreads as there is chicken. Heat through quickly, not allowing the mixture to boil. Just before taking up add one teaspoonful of well-washed parsley, chopped fine. Serve on a hot platter in a border of green peas.

Chicken or Turkey Timbale with or without Mushroom Sauce

When no more slices can be cut from a cooked chicken or turkey, take the bits of meat near the bones, chop fine, and to two cups of such meat allow one cup of soft, white bread-crumbs and one-half cup of hot milk. Mix the crumbs and hot milk together, then add the chopped meat and yolks of two eggs. Season with one teaspoonful of salt and one-quarter teaspoonful of pepper. Beat the whites *slightly*—they must not be frothy—and mix them well in. Turn the mixture into a buttered pan or mold, cover with a greased paper, and steam; or set in pan of hot water and cook in moderate oven about one hour. Carefully unmold on a hot platter, and serve with or without mushroom sauce (see page 69).

Hotel Club Sandwiches

Cut the bread about one-half inch in thickness. Toast it a delicate brown, and butter it slightly. Lay thin slices of chicken on the toast, then a crisp leaf of lettuce, a few strips of very thin broiled bacon, and a little mayonnaise dressing (see page

POULTRY

74). Cover with another slice of toast, and serve at once.

A Scallop of Chicken with Celery

Cook one cup of celery, cut in inch pieces, in boiling slightly salted water, until tender. Save the water to make sauce. There should be one cup. Slice thin two cups of cold chicken, discarding all skin, season with salt and pepper, and moisten with a little left-over gravy. Melt two tablespoonfuls of butter, stir in two tablespoonfuls of flour, and when bubbling add slowly one cup of celery water, one-half cup of milk, one-quarter teaspoonful of salt, and a little pepper. When thickened and smooth, stir in the cooked celery. Put a few buttered crumbs in a baking-dish and arrange the chicken and sauce in alternate layers. Cover with well-buttered crumbs. Brown in a hot oven.

Chicken Croquettes

To be creamy inside these must be made very soft, then the mixture set away to cool and stiffen before it is shaped into croquettes. Make a white sauce No. 4 (see page 68). Chop the chicken fine and season—with salt, pepper, grated lemon rind, a few drops of onion-juice, grating of nutmeg, and a little mace. Put into the hot sauce all the seasoned chicken it will take up, about two cups to one of sauce. Set away to cool. Then shape into croquettes, roll in fine bread-crumbs, then in egg (which has been slightly beaten together with one tablespoonful of cold water), being careful to have every part covered with egg, then in crumbs again. Fry in smoking deep fat, and serve with white sauce No. 2 (see page 68). Veal or fresh pork may be used instead of chicken.

Creamed Chicken with Asparagus Tips

Any kind of cooked chicken can be used for this. Discard all skin and hard portions. Cut the meat in half-inch pieces. Season with salt, pepper, and one teaspoonful of lemon-juice to one cup of meat. Add one-half cup of chicken stock—made from bones, wing ends, and the like, and simmer gently together ten minutes, then add one-half cup of canned or cooked asparagus tips to each cup of chicken, and let heat. Make half a cup of white sauce No. 2 (see page 68). When the sauce is cooked, stir in one egg yolk beaten with one teaspoonful of water, and remove from the fire at once. Add this to the hot chicken and serve immediately. Garnish the platter with triangles of well-browned toast.

Minced Chicken and Ham in Tomato Cases

6 tomatoes	2 tablespoonfuls of melted butter
½ cup minced chicken	½ teaspoonful of pepper
¼ cup minced ham	
¾ cup fresh bread-crumbs	½ teaspoonful of mustard
2 teaspoonfuls of salt	

Select uniform tomatoes of medium size. Cut a slice from the stem end and carefully remove the pulp with a spoon. Mix all ingredients well together with the tomato pulp. Season the inside of the tomato cases with salt and a very little sugar, and fill them with the mixture. Put a piece of butter on top of each. Bake in an agate pan

POULTRY

in a hot oven about fifteen minutes. The cases should be cooked until tender, but not broken.

Chicken Soufflé

Season one cup of white sauce No. 3 (see page **68**) with parsley, a little thyme, and onion. Add one cup of chopped chicken, or a mixture of veal and chicken, or chicken and a little tender ham. While hot add the beaten yolks of two eggs, or three, if eggs are plentiful. Let it cool, then cut and fold into the mixture the whites of the eggs beaten stiff. Put into a buttered dish, and bake about twenty minutes in a hot oven. Serve at once.

Chicken Hash

1½ cups cold chopped chicken	¾ cup boiled potatoes ½ to ⅔ cup chicken gravy

Cut the potatoes in small pieces. Mix together, season highly, and moisten with the chicken gravy. Butter some ramekins or small bowls, put in the mixture, covering the top with a very thin layer of fine buttered crumbs. Sprinkle a teaspoonful of milk over the crumbs, and on the top of each ramekin lay a slice of raw tomato. A bit of butter on the tomato helps to brown it. Bake for about fifteen minutes in a hot oven. The tomato should be soft and the crumbs well browned.

Chicken Tamale Dressing

1 cup corn-meal	1 cup cooked chicken, chopped fine
1 tablespoonful butter or bacon fat	1 cup stoned olives
1 tablespoonful onion-juice	4 tablespoonfuls catsup
1 cup tomatoes	Cayenne pepper
3 tablespoonfuls oil	Salt

Scald the corn-meal with about one cup of boiling water, add the other ingredients in the order given. Put in a buttered dish and bake half an hour.

This is a favorite California dish.

Chicken Pie (from Cooked Chicken)

Cut the meat from the drumsticks, disjoint and use the wings, the second joints, neck, and any other pieces. The presence of these small bones adds flavor to the pie. Put into a suitable baking-dish, season the chicken well, and pour over it one and one-third cups of thickened gravy, which can be made from the water in which the chicken was cooked. Cover with a pastry crust made of

1 cup flour	1/4 cup ice-water
1/4 cup shortening, part chicken and part beef fat	1 teaspoonful salt
	1/2 teaspoonful baking-powder

Sift the flour, salt, and baking-powder together. Chop in the fat, moisten with ice-water, and roll out. Put bits of butter over the crust, using a tablespoonful, sprinkle with a little flour, and roll up like a jelly roll. Let stand in the ice-box until ready to use for the pie. When rolling out the crust, make several slits in it that the steam may escape. It is considered an advantage to have a cup in the bottom of the dish to collect the gravy.

Boneless Birds

Cut into small pieces cold roast veal, chicken, or any left-over meat. Season highly. Roll a heaping tablespoonful of the cut meat in a slice of bacon, pinning the bacon together with a slender wooden toothpick. Bake these on a tin in a hot oven about fifteen minutes, basting and turning the "birds." Serve hot on a garnished platter. A very good luncheon dish. They should be as large as a croquette when served.

Victoria Meat (from Chicken or Veal)

3 teaspoonfuls butter	¼ teaspoonful salt
3 teaspoonfuls flour	Paprika
2 slices onion	Bay leaf
4 mushrooms	½ cup tomato-juice
1 cup stock	1½ cups meat, cut in small cubes
1 cup drained peas	

Melt butter, stir in flour, salt, paprika, bay leaf and onion; add stock and tomato-juice gradually, stirring constantly. When slightly thickened add mushrooms cut in pieces, meat, and peas. Reheat on stove and serve in croustades. This dish requires good stock.

Chicken-and-Rice Soufflé-scallop

1 cup chicken	Gravy
½ cup boiled rice	1 egg white, beaten very light
½ cup white sauce No. 1 (see page 67)	Bread-crumbs
1 egg yolk, beaten	Bits of butter
Salt and paprika	

Mix chicken, rice, gravy, seasoning, and yolk of egg. Make white sauce; while hot add chicken mixture. Cool slightly, fold in white of egg, put into buttered baking-dish, cover with bread-crumbs and bits of butter. Bake half an hour.

THE COOK BOOK OF LEFT-OVERS

Chicken Gumbo Soup (West Indian)

Chicken stock, seasoned	3 tomatoes
	1 carrot
6 or 8 okras sliced thin	2 ears of corn
¼ onion cut in pieces	Pieces of cooked chicken
2 teaspoonfuls butter	

Cook carrot sliced in straws in small amount of water, letting the water boil down. Simmer together (covered) okras, onion, and butter for fifteen minutes. Add tomatoes cut in pieces, and cook until soft, then add the cooked carrot and carrot liquid. Put these vegetables into the stock (of which there should be about one and a half quarts), and cook together until all are tender. Fifteen minutes before serving put in corn, which has been scored and scraped from cob. Finally add chicken. Heat almost to boiling, and serve.

Cream of Rice and Chicken Soup

Chicken bones should be covered with three pints cold water. Let boil up for a few minutes, then simmer until stock is reduced to a pint. Melt one tablespoonful butter; when bubbling add one tablespoonful flour, one salt-spoonful salt, a little nutmeg and cayenne. Pour in stock gradually, let boil up, add one-fourth (or one-third) cup cooked rice and a little of the thick rice water in which it was cooked, if this has been saved. When well heated add half a cup of cream and the grated yolk of one hard-cooked egg.

Chicken Custard

When boiling a fowl for salad or other purposes take a pint of the broth. Season as needed with

POULTRY

salt and a little pepper. Heat and pour very slowly over two eggs that have been slightly beaten: Cook in a double boiler until the mixture thickens Pour into small cups that have been rinsed with cold water and set away to chill. This makes a good relish for an invalid.

Duckling Stew

Bones and meat left from a pair of roast ducklings	4 small boiled potatoes cut in cubes
3 small onions	Few stoned olives
3 or 4 small carrots cut in slices or cubes	Gravy
	Flour
	Seasonings

Cut the carcasses of ducks into suitable pieces. Melt in stew-pan some of fat skimmed from leftover gravy, add flour, and when hot put in the ducks and heat through thoroughly. Gradually add hot water and gizzard gravy cooked the day before. When sufficient water has been added for stock, put in onions, carrots, a bay leaf, two cloves, a little salt and pepper and dash of cayenne. Simmer for one or more hours, uncovering stew occasionally to turn pieces in stock. Add gravy gradually, then the olives, and twenty minutes before serving, the potatoes. Serve with currant jelly.

Chicken in Batter

See Veal in Batter, page 35.

Chicken-Liver Sandwiches

See page 231.

MY OWN RECEIPTS

MY OWN RECEIPTS

MY OWN RECEIPTS

MY OWN RECEIPTS

MY OWN RECEIPTS

SAUCES

Most made-over dishes are dependent upon some kind of a sauce to make them acceptable; it is therefore quite essential that the cook be familiar with the simple foundation sauces. This knowledge gained, it is an easy matter to prepare any of the more elaborate ones.

A good sauce is always perfectly smooth and properly flavored. The smoothness is secured by drawing the saucepan from the high heat and adding the liquid slowly to the blended flour and fat, beating and stirring constantly until the sauce thickens. The flavoring is best secured by utilizing all odd bits of meat, fish, bones, and vegetables to make savory stock, or by cooking a few chopped vegetables carefully in the fat and removing them before the flour is added.

The use of potato flour for sauces, in the same proportions as wheat flour, is recommended, as it gives excellent results with much less cooking.

All measures of butter should be level.

White Sauce No. 1 (for Omelets, Cream Soups, Toast)

1 tablespoonful butter
1 tablespoonful flour
1 cup milk
¼ teaspoonful salt
⅛ teaspoonful white pepper

White Sauce No. 1 A (for Scalloped Dishes and Omelets)

1½ tablespoonfuls butter
1½ tablespoonfuls flour
¼ teaspoonful salt
⅛ teaspoonful white pepper
1 cup milk

White Sauce No. 2 (for Creamed Meats, Fish, Vegetables, Toast)

2 tablespoonfuls butter
2 tablespoonfuls flour
¼ teaspoonful salt
⅛ teaspoonful white pepper
1 cup milk

White Sauce No. 3 (for Soufflés)

3 tablespoonfuls butter
3 tablespoonfuls flour
¼ teaspoonful salt
⅛ teaspoonful white pepper
1 cup milk

White Sauce No. 4 (for Croquettes)

4 tablespoonfuls butter
4 tablespoonfuls flour
¼ teaspoonful salt
⅛ teaspoonful white pepper
1 cup milk

Melt the butter, stir in the flour and seasoning and cook slowly without browning until the mixture bubbles. Remove from the high heat, add the milk gradually, beating and stirring constantly until the sauce thickens.

Vegetable Sauce

This may be made from either celery, asparagus, cauliflower, green peas or mushrooms. One-half

SAUCES

cup of any one of these vegetables may be added to one cup of white sauce No. 2. Serve with chicken, meat, or fish croquettes.

Mushroom Sauce

Melt one tablespoonful of butter, add one tablespoonful of flour, and when bubbling stir in slowly one cup of rich milk, beating constantly until the sauce thickens. Season with one-quarter teaspoonful of salt, a dash of cayenne, and a little celery salt. Add one-half can of chopped mushrooms.

Egg Sauce

Place two eggs in rapidly boiling water, cover tightly, remove to cooler part of stove, and let stand six minutes. The whites should be solid and yolks soft. Beat in the soft yolks and add the chopped whites to one cup of white sauce No. 2. Just before serving add one teaspoonful chopped parsley. Serve with boiled fish.

Cheese Sauce

Add one-half cup of grated cheese to one cup of white sauce No. 2. Use paprika instead of pepper in making the sauce.

Poulette Sauce

2 tablespoonfuls butter	$\frac{1}{4}$ teaspoonful salt
2 tablespoonfuls flour	$\frac{1}{8}$ teaspoonful white pepper
$\frac{1}{4}$ cup sweet cream	1 egg yolk
1 cup white stock	A little nutmeg
1 tablespoonful lemon-juice	

THE COOK BOOK OF LEFT-OVERS

Melt butter, add flour and seasonings; when bubbling stir in white stock. Make the white stock from any bones or odd bits of chicken or veal by covering with cold water, add a little chopped celery or carrot and one bay leaf, simmer slowly for two hours, then strain. When thickened, add slowly the beaten yolk, cream, and nutmeg. Heat all together, but do not boil. Just before serving add the lemon-juice carefully. Especially acceptable with warmed-over chicken or veal.

Drawn Butter Sauce

4 tablespoonfuls butter
2 tablespoonfuls flour
1 cup water
¼ teaspoonful salt
⅛ teaspoonful white pepper

Melt two tablespoonfuls of the butter, add flour and seasoning, and cook until mixture bubbles. Add the water slowly, beat and stir until sauce thickens. Remove from fire and beat in the rest of the butter slowly. A few chopped cucumber pickles added to this sauce makes it appetizing with warmed-over fish.

Caper Sauce

To one cup of drawn butter sauce add two tablespoonfuls of capers.

Brown Sauce

2 tablespoonfuls butter
2 tablespoonfuls flour
A small slice of onion
1 cup brown stock
¼ teaspoonful salt
⅛ teaspoonful pepper

Melt butter, put in onion, and when slightly browned, the flour. Cook together until a little

SAUCES

darker in color. Pour in stock gradually, as in directions given for adding milk to white sauces (see page 68). Let boil one minute and strain.

Note: A few drops of kitchen bouquet will darken sauces and gravies when the butter and flour have not been sufficiently browned at first.

Olive Sauce

Drain, rinse in cold water and dry eight medium-sized olives. Chop them fine and add to the above brown sauce just before serving.

Savory Tomato Sauce (for Chops and Fish)

2 tablespoonfuls butter	½ teaspoonful salt
2 tablespoonfuls flour	2 sprigs parsley
6 peppercorns	1 slice of onion
6 cloves	3 large tomatoes
	A bit of bay leaf

Scald, peel, and cut tomatoes in pieces. Put with them a tablespoonful of water and stew until soft enough to measure. To one and a half cups (if tomato has boiled down to less, add thin stock or hot water to make up deficiency) add the spice and seasoning. Boil all together fifteen minutes. Strain and add gradually to flour and butter cooked together. Boil up one minute and serve

Mock Bisque Sauce—with Cheese

1 lb. tomatoes (3 medium-sized)	1½ tablespoonfuls butter
½ cup soup celery	2 tablespoonfuls flour
½ teaspoonful salt	½ cup scalded milk
⅛ tablespoonful white pepper	1 or 2 tablespoonfuls dry American cheese (grated)

Wash celery and tomatoes well, put on to cook with one tablespoonful of water and boil slowly fifteen minutes. Put through a strainer fine enough to hold back the seeds. Melt the butter, add the flour, pepper, and salt, and, when well blended, the tomato, of which there should be half a cup. Let boil up well, remove from heat, and slowly stir in the hot milk. Keep the sauce hot, but do not allow it to boil after adding milk. Stir into it while on the stove the grated cheese. When this is melted the sauce is ready for the table. A good sauce for macaroni or spaghetti, plain boiled rice served as a vegetable, or for rice croquettes.

Hollandaise Sauce

½ cup butter
6 tablespoonfuls boiling water
4 egg yolks
1 tablespoonful lemon-juice or vinegar
Salt and cayenne

Cream the butter, add egg yolks, and stir vigorously. Then add lemon-juice, seasoning, and water. Beat five minutes with Dover egg beater. Cook over hot water, and continue to stir until thickened.

Cold Sauces and Dressings

A good oil should be used in making salad dressings, but it is not necessary to pay the highest price for it. An excellent quality of olive oil may be purchased at some of the small Italian shops for a reasonable amount. This low price is made possible since it is their own importation.

SAUCES

There is also now on the market a good domestic oil prepared from cotton seed. It is largely used instead of the imported oil, and an excellent mayonnaise can be made from it.

French Dressing No. 1

 1 tablespoonful vinegar
 3 tablespoonfuls oil
 ½ teaspoonful salt
 White pepper

This is the usual proportion of oil and vinegar but an equal quantity of each may be used if desired, or more oil.[1]

To the seasoning in a bowl add the oil and vinegar, and beat with Dover beater or fork until it thickens slightly. Use at once. When made at the table the dressing will thicken more quickly if a bit of ice is put in the bowl with the other ingredients. Remove ice when dressing is made.

French Dressing No. 2

 2 tablespoonfuls oil
 2 tablespoonfuls vinegar
 1 tablespoonful beaten egg
 ½ teaspoonful salt
 A little pepper

Put all together into a bowl and beat with a Dover egg beater. Pour over the salad just before it is sent to the table.

---

[1] In France they say to add the vinegar to salad dressing in the time one can say very quickly, *Ners* (a French railway station), but the oil is poured in while one is saying, very slowly, *Saint—Jean—de—Maurienne*

Mayonnaise Dressing

½ teaspoonful powdered sugar
¼ teaspoonful dry mustard
¼ teaspoonful salt
Yolk of 1 raw egg
½ to ⅔ cup salad oil
2 tablespoonfuls lemon-juice
A very little cayenne pepper

Put all the dry ingredients into a bowl. Mix and add the yolk of an egg. Beat all together with a silver fork until thickened, then add the lemon-juice little by little, beating it in. Then put in the oil a teaspoonful at a time, beating well with a small Dover egg beater between each addition of oil. Oil and egg should be very cold.

This dressing may be made thicker by using two-thirds of a cup of oil instead of one-half. Two tablespoonfuls of thick, sweet cream may be stirred into it as an addition.

Sauce Tartare

This sauce is made like the above dressing, with the addition of chopped capers, olives, pickles, and parsley. Omit the cream.

Maître d'Hôtel Butter (for Steak and Broiled Fish)

3 tablespoonfuls butter
1 teaspoonful lemon-juice
1 full teaspoonful finely chopped parsley

Cream the butter well, gradually beat in the lemon-juice, and finally add the chopped parsley. Spread over the hot steak or fish just before serving.

SAUCES

Cooked Salad Dressing

- 3 egg yolks, well beaten
- 2 tablespoonfuls butter
- 1½ teaspoonfuls mustard
- 3 tablespoonfuls boiling vinegar
- 1 teaspoonful sugar
- Cream or unsweetened condensed milk
- ½ teaspoonful salt

Add the boiling vinegar slowly to the eggs. Cook over hot water until thickened, stirring constantly. Mix mustard, sugar, and salt, and add. Beat in the butter. This will keep in a cool place for a long time. When ready to use add an equal bulk of sweet or sour cream, or unsweetened condensed milk.

Mustard Sauce

Brown lightly together half a tablespoonful of butter and half a tablespoonful of flour. Add slowly a quarter of a cup of hot water. Beat well. When thick and smooth, stir in half a tablespoonful lemon juice, a little salt and cayenne, and one scant teaspoonful of mixed mustard. Then beat in slowly two tablespoonfuls of cream.

Sour Cream Dressing (for Vegetable Salads)

Mash one hard-cooked egg yolk with half a teaspoonful of butter until very smooth and creamy. Season with salt, paprika, a little mustard, and two tablespoonfuls of lemon juice. Beat in four tablespoonfuls of sour cream, or any unsweetened condensed milk that may have soured.

MY OWN RECEIPTS

MY OWN RECEIPTS

MY OWN RECEIPTS

MY OWN RECEIPTS

MY OWN RECEIPTS

WHAT TO DO WITH LEFT-OVER FISH

Fish, like meat, is particularly attractive to flies, therefore any cooked remnants should be carefully screened while cooling, and never placed in contact with butter or milk in the ice-box. It should be reheated within twenty-four hours of the first cooking. Like tender meat, the fiber of fish is hardened by continuous high heat, therefore great care should be taken in reheating it.

Boiled Fish in Potato Border

2 cups cooked fish, flaked
2 cups hot or cold mashed potato
hard cooked eggs
cup drawn butter sauce (see page 70)
1 tablespoonful minced parsley

Press the two cups of well-seasoned mashed potato through a ricer, letting it fall lightly around the edge of a flat baking-platter to form a border. In the center of the dish put alternate layers of fish, sliced eggs, and sauce, sprinkling each layer with a very little minced parsley. Place in a hot oven until sauce bubbles. Serve in the baking-platter.

Spiced Fish with White Sauce

Season highly any left-over boiled white fish with one of the following, or a combination: tomato catsup, anchovy, Worcestershire, and a little paprika. Make enough white sauce No. 3 (see page 68) to cover the fish, adding two well-beaten egg yolks to each cup of sauce. Flake the fish, pour the sauce over and heat in oven.

Clam Broth

When frying or making a scallop of soft clams it is unwise to put in the long, hard neck portions, for they are not eaten. Use these for broth. Put them through a meat chopper, with a few whole clams, add a little water, salt as needed, and a little pepper. Simmer gently for a few minutes, strain, and serve hot or cold. This is an excellent tonic.

Fish Cocktail

Take a small piece of cold boiled halibut, remove the skin and bones and flake it. Season it with salt and a little pepper. Make a cocktail sauce by mixing together for each glass

1 teaspoonful Tarragon vinegar	1 teaspoonful lemon-juice
1 teaspoonful tomato catsup	½ teaspoonful of horse-radish
1 drop Tabasco sauce	

Take about a tablespoonful of fish for each portion, put in a glass, and pour the sauce over.

Cold Fish with Cold Hollandaise Sauce

Arrange slices of any cold boiled fish on a platter. Cover them with slices of hard-cooked

FISH

eggs which have been seasoned with salt and pepper. Remove the bones and rub two or three sardines to a smooth paste. Add them to any left-over Hollandaise sauce (see page 72). When ready to serve pour the sauce over the fish and sprinkle a few chopped capers over all.

Creamed Fish

Make as much white sauce No. 2 (see page 68) as there is flaked fish, and add a slight grating of nutmeg. Season the fish well with salt and pepper, and add to the hot sauce, together with a few spoonfuls of cooked green peas, and serve as soon as heated.

Fish with Creamed Oysters

A little left-over boiled fish and a few creamed oysters arranged in ramekins with any white or drawn butter sauce (see pages 67-70), covered with buttered crumbs and browned in oven, make an acceptable luncheon dish.

Fish and Cheese Soufflé

See page 169.

Baked Chowder

3 raw potatoes, sliced very thin	1½ cups boiled fish
2 small onions, sliced thin	3 slices of cooked bacon and bacon fat
1 cup stewed tomatoes	Salt and pepper
1 cup water	

In a buttered baking-dish arrange alternate layers of potatoes, onions, tomatoes, and fish, seasoning each layer with salt and pepper and a little of the bacon crushed fine, and the bacon fat. Moisten with the water, dredge the top with flour, and bake covered until the potatoes are soft, then uncover and brown.

Mock Lobster in Chafing-dish

1½ cups boiled fish, preferably salmon	1 tablespoonful butter
1 cup stewed tomatoes well seasoned	Salt, paprika, and a little Worcestershire sauce
2 tablespoonfuls cracker crumbs	1 tablespoonful butter

Melt the butter in the chafing-dish, add the tomatoes, fish, seasoning, and crumbs. Heat all well together.

Boston Scalloped Fish

2½ cups cold flaked haddock or halibut	⅔ cup cracker-crumbs, buttered
	⅛ teaspoonful pepper
1½ cups white sauce No. 1 (see page 67), or drawn butter sauce (p. 70)	½ teaspoonful salt
	1 tablespoonful butter

Put one-half of the fish in the bottom of a well-buttered baking-dish, add seasoning and small bits of butter. Cover with cracker-crumbs and pour over half of the sauce. Repeat and cover the top with a few crumbs, and brown in hot oven.

Baked Fish in Pepper Cases

Carefully remove the skin and bones from any baked fish and season it with salt, pepper, and a

FISH

little onion juice. Mix with it an equal quantity of left-over stuffing, or coarse crumbs moistened with butter. The mixture should be quite moist; if not, add a little fish stock or milk. Cut lengthwise as many green sweet peppers as needed, remove seeds, parboil five minutes, and fill them with the fish. Put them in an agate baking-pan, surround with hot fish stock or boiling water half an inch deep, and cook until cases are soft, but not broken.

Fish Loaf

Flake the remnants of any baked fish. There should be two cups; if not, fill out with raw oysters. Add one cup of stuffing left from the fish, or one cup of coarse bread crumbs moistened with melted butter, and one beaten egg. Season well with salt, pepper, and one teaspoonful finely minced pickle. Turn into a small bread-pan or quart mold, cover with buttered paper, place in pan of hot water and cook in moderate oven about half an hour. Unmold on a hot platter and serve with white sauce No. 2 (see page 68), adding one-quarter cup cooked peas to the sauce.

Fish with Mushrooms

1 cup fish	1 cup white sauce No. 2 (see page 68)
1 tablespoonful chopped onion	1 tablespoonful butter
1½ cups button mushrooms	2 tablespoonfuls grated cheese

Baked or boiled fish can be used. Flake the fish, cut the mushrooms in halves and cook until tender (canned ones may be used). Brown the onion lightly in the butter and add fish, white sauce, and mushrooms. Place in ramekins, cover top with grated cheese, and heat in oven until cheese melts.

Creamed Fish in Potato Cups

Discard all bones and skin from any boiled or fried fish. Season well with salt, pepper, and a little lemon-juice. Make white sauce No. 3 (see page 68), allowing half as much sauce as fish. Add a slight grating of nutmeg to the sauce and add fish to it. Put the mixture in potato cups and brown lightly in oven.

Potato Cups

These are easily made by adding one egg yolk to one cup well-seasoned mashed potato. The potato should be slightly warm. This amount will make four cups. Invert any custard cups or jelly-glasses and cover the outside, bottom and two inches up the sides with the potato mixture. Smooth over and set away to get cold. When ready to use turn right side up on a well-buttered flat pan and very carefully remove the molds. Brush the outside with beaten egg and milk before adding the fish.

Fresh Fish Cakes

Any kind of cooked fish can be used for these. It should be shredded fine and highly seasoned with salt, pepper, and a little Worcestershire sauce, if liked. Moisten dry fish, such as fresh cod or haddock, with a little melted butter. Mix the fish with an equal quantity of mashed potato. The best results are obtained when the potato is

FISH

freshly mashed, seasoned well with salt, butter, a little cream or rich milk, and one egg yolk added to each cup of potato. Beat the mixture until light before adding the fish. Form into flat cakes and brown in a little salt pork fat.

Fish Balls Baked

1 cup cooked fish, flaked
1 cup cold rice
1 egg
1 tablespoonful club cheese
1 teaspoonful lemon-juice
Salt and pepper

Beat the egg until light, then add fish, rice, cheese, and seasoning. Form into small balls, place in a buttered pan and bake to a delicate brown. Serve on slices of buttered toast with tomato sauce (see page 71).

Fish Salad in Green Peppers

Cut lengthwise three or four green sweet peppers, remove the seeds and set away to chill. Discard all skin and bones from any cold boiled fish and pick apart into suitable sized pieces for salad. Season it with salt and pepper as needed, and sprinkle with a little lemon-juice. When ready to prepare the salad, mix the fish with enough mayonnaise (see page 74) or cold Hollandaise sauce (see page 72) to cover it well. Fill the peppers with this mixture, letting it fall in lightly, and garnish the top of each with a slice of hard-cooked egg. This makes a good Saturday luncheon dish in warm weather.

Shad-Roe Salad

When the shad roe is not needed for the fish dinner a salad can be made of it for the next day's luncheon. It spoils quickly, so should be cooked promptly. If not baked with the fish, put the roe in slightly salted boiling water and simmer gently for about fifteen minutes. Drain and wipe dry. Dip in beaten egg, roll in fine white bread-crumbs, and brown lightly in a little butter. While still warm pour over it two tablespoonfuls lemon-juice and season with salt and a little paprika. Set away to chill. When ready to serve cut it in suitable-sized pieces and mix with it an equal quantity of very crisp cucumber cubes. Cover with a mayonnaise dressing (see page 74) and decorate the top with capers and chopped olives. Serve on crisp lettuce-leaves. This salad should be prepared just before serving.

Jellied Fish

In summer cold fish is quite as acceptable as warm, and a luncheon dish can easily be prepared by mixing one and one-half cups of any well-seasoned cold flaked fish with two tablespoonfuls of chopped capers. Soak one tablespoonful of granulated gelatine in two tablespoonfuls of cold water for half an hour. Add one cup of boiling water and stir until the gelatine dissolves. Then add two tablespoonfuls of lemon-juice and a little salt. Put slices of hard-cooked eggs in the bottom of an earthen mold holding about a quart, and add the fish. Pour the jelly carefully over all and put on ice to harden. Garnish a platter with watercress or lettuce and turn the mold out on this. It must be served at once after unmolding. Use any kind of salad dressing, or sauce Tartare (see page 74).

FISH

Kedjeree

1 cup left-over smoked fish	1 scant cup cooked rice
2 hard-cooked eggs	2 tablespoonfuls butter
Seasoning	

Cook eggs hard, or if any soft-cooked ones are left from breakfast steam them until hard. Carefully take out the bones from the fish and chop it up with the eggs. Reheat cooked rice, having it a little moist. When it is very hot put in the fish, eggs, and butter, and heat all up together. Add paprika, salt if necessary, and serve very hot. Smoked haddock or white fish recommended for this dish.

Fish Mélange

1 cup cold boiled fish (cod, halibut, salmon, etc.)	1 cup white sauce No.1 (see page 67)
2 cups riced potato	2 tablespoonfuls butter
Cayenne	Salt and white pepper

Flake fish, add potato, and beat as for mashed potatoes, adding butter, salt, and white pepper. Mix with white sauce seasoned with a dash of cayenne, put into a buttered porcelain dish, dot with bits of butter and bake until brown.

Fish and Potato Salad

Use for this salad any left-over white fish, baked, boiled, broiled, or sautéd, being careful to remove all bones. For each cup of flaked fish use one cup of potatoes cut in dice. Mix with French dressing No. 1 (see page 73), pouring it over fish and potato separately. If potato is freshly boiled and *warm* when dressing is added, seasoning will penetrate potato more easily, giving better flavor. When ready to put salad together, drain off any excess of liquid, add chopped sweet red peppers (canned), and mix carefully, that potato may keep its shape. Season more highly if necessary. Serve in individual portions on crisp lettuce-leaves, putting a spoonful of mayonnaise dressing (see page 84) on top of each. Garnish with narrow strips of red peppers.

Oyster Bisque

When creaming oysters, if the juice is not used, save it and make a bisque for the next meal. (It should not be kept long.) Melt two tablespoonfuls of butter, add two tablespoonfuls flour and stir until smooth. Add one cup of boiling water and one cup of strained oyster-juice. Season with salt and pepper and let boil. Mix beaten yolk of one egg with one-quarter cup of cream; add hot mixture to this slowly, stirring briskly. Serve at once. Chicken stock, if at hand, may be substituted for part or all of the water.

Salmon Canapés

Small pieces of white or rye bread can be profitably utilized by cutting them into neat round or oblong shapes, browning in fat in a frying-pan, and spreading with a canapé mixture made by rubbing some bits of smoked salmon to a smooth paste, mixing it with one tablespoonful of mixed mustard, one tablespoonful of Tarragon vinegar, one tablespoonful of finely chopped green sweet peppers,

FISH

and one-half tablespoonful of finely minced capers. Serve these at the beginning of a luncheon or a dinner.

Salmon Soup

The remnants of any canned or boiled salmon may be used for this. Pick the fish apart and moisten with the liquor in the can and a little warm water, or water in which the fish was boiled. Press it through a purée strainer. There should be one cup fish pulp and liquid. Season with salt and pepper as needed. Make two cups of white sauce No. 1 (see page 67), add the fish, and heat together, but do not boil. Just before serving add a little well-washed and finely minced parsley, or a tablespoonful of hot green peas. If too thick, thin with a little hot milk.

Salmon Croquettes

¾ cup boiled or canned salmon
½ cup white sauce No. 4 (see page 68)
½ cup green peas
½ tablespoonful lemon-juice
Salt, pepper, dash nutmeg

Flake the fish, season with salt and pepper as needed, and sprinkle with lemon-juice. Add nutmeg to white sauce, and mix fish, sauce, and peas together. Set away to get very cold. Shape, roll in fine white crumbs, dip carefully in slightly beaten egg and roll again in crumbs. Fry in deep fat. If the mixture should be too soft to shape add a few cracker-crumbs. Press the peas through a wire strainer without any liquid, as they need to be very stiff. Season well with salt and pepper. Serve the croquettes with sauce Tartare (see page 74).

Salmon Loaf

1½ cups cold cooked salmon (fresh or canned)
¾ cup bread-crumbs
3 eggs, well beaten
3 tablespoonfuls melted butter
Salt and pepper

Mix well and steam one hour. Serve with dressing (see below).

Special Dressing for Salmon Loaf

1 cup milk
1 scant tablespoonful corn-starch
1 well-beaten egg
1 teaspoonful butter
Salt and pepper

Heat milk, add corn-starch blended with cold water, and cook together one minute, or until sauce boils. Combine with egg, cook slightly, add salt, pepper, and butter. Pour over loaf and serve hot or cold.

Salmon Salad

Season large pieces of left-over salmon with vinegar, salt, and pepper. When ready to use, drain off liquid, place in center of platter on lettuce, and surround with any one or two, or all of the following vegetables: string-beans, asparagus tips, peas, beets, tomatoes (less of this than of the others). Use lettuce leaves as a border. Serve with mayonnaise or French dressing (see pages 73-74).

Salmon Scallop

Butter a baking-dish and put in alternate layers of bread-crumbs and cooked flaked salmon, having bottom and top layer crumbs. Season with salt and pepper, fill up dish with milk, dot bits of butter over top, and bake. Left-over baked bluefish may be used in the same way.

A Breakfast Relish of Smoked Salmon

A few very thin slices of smoked salmon, dipped in boiling water and placed on rounds of browned and buttered toast, one slice on each round, and a poached egg slipped on top, make an appetizing breakfast dish.

Creamed Codfish and Macaroni

Heat one cup of creamed salt codfish with one cup of cooked macaroni, or macaroni and cheese, adding more cream or milk if necessary. Serve in a border of scrambled eggs. This makes an excellent breakfast relish.

Codfish Scallop with Rice and Eggs

1½ cups creamed codfish
1½ cups boiled rice
2 tablespoonfuls cream or 1 tablespoonful butter
4 eggs

Mix the cream or melted butter with the rice and arrange alternate layers of fish and rice in a buttered quart baking-dish, finishing with rice. Carefully break four eggs on top, season the whites with salt, and sprinkle with a little cream or dot with butter. Bake in oven until heated and eggs "set," or individual ramekins may be used and an egg slipped on top of each.

Fish with Pie Crust

Line a baking-tin with a good pastry crust and bake it. Remove all bones and skin from any cold boiled white fish and flake it. There should be two cups; if not, fill out with a few raw oysters. Season as needed with salt and pepper. Make quite moist with drawn butter sauce (see page 70), or white sauce No. 2 (see page 68), reserving enough sauce to cover top. Spread the mixture on the baked crust. Cover with a layer of thin slices of hard-cooked eggs, season with salt and pepper, and pour over the remaining sauce. Sprinkle with buttered crumbs and brown in hot oven.

Fish Hash

1 cup any kind of white fish
1 cup diced potatoes
1 hard-cooked egg
1 teaspoonful mixed mustard
1 tablespoonful green sweet pepper, shredded
2 tablespoonfuls melted butter
½ cup milk
Salt, pepper

Flake the fish, add seasoning, chop the egg, toss the potatoes in the melted butter, and mix all together. Melt a little extra butter in a frying-pan, and when hot add the mixture, cover, and cook slowly until all is well blended, then uncover and brown on bottom. Fold over and turn out on a warm platter.

Stuffed Peppers with Crab Meat

Cut a slice from the stem-end of as many green sweet peppers as needed, remove seeds and parti-

FISH

tion walls and parboil for five minutes. Brush the inside of each with melted butter and fill with a mixture made of equal quantities of cooked rice and cold crab meat. Moisten the rice with a little sweet cream and add one tablespoonful of grated cheese to a cup of rice. Season the crab meat with salt, paprika, and a few drops of lemon-juice. Mix all lightly together and have it quite moist. Place the peppers in an agate baking-pan, surround with boiling water, adding half a tablespoonful of butter to half a cup of water. Baste now and then. Cook about fifteen minutes.

Scallop of Fried Fish with Fresh Tomatoes

Remove the skin and bones from any kind of fried fish. Season highly, adding Worcestershire if liked. Arrange in a buttered baking-dish in alternate layers with peeled and sliced fresh tomatoes. Season tomatoes well with salt, pepper, and dots of butter. Cover top with well-buttered cracker-crumbs. Cook in a moderate oven until tomatoes are quite soft and crumbs browned.

Broiled Sardines on Toast

Prepare pieces of toast, moistening with butter melted in hot water. Broil sardines until well heated through, place on toast on platter, and garnish with parsley and slices of lemon.

Sardines with Tomato Catsup

Cook sardines in pan slightly. Heat catsup and pour over them. Serve on crackers.

THE COOK BOOK OF LEFT-OVERS

Toasted Sardine Sandwiches

Cut thin slices of white bread into squares, triangles, or rounds. Remove bones and skin from sardines, add lemon-juice and a dash of cayenne to the fish. Spread bread lightly with butter, then with the sardine mixture and toast a delicate brown. Serve very hot. A good dish for Sunday night supper.

Luncheon Relish of Sardines

Dip slices of cold hominy in milk and eggs beaten together. Lay them in a buttered pan and put one sardine on each slice. Brown lightly in a hot oven.

MY OWN RECEIPTS

MY OWN RECEIPTS

MY OWN RECEIPTS

MY OWN RECEIPTS

WHAT TO DO WITH LEFT-OVER VEGETABLES

During warm weather, when vegetables are most abundant, great care should be taken not to allow them to accumulate in the ice-box or pantry, as they spoil quickly after being cooked. As a general rule, they are not injured, either in digestibility or flavor, by reheating, and as they are an expensive item in the food bill, especially in cities, they should never be wasted. Even a spoonful or two of almost any cooked vegetable will help to flavor a soup or sauce.

Dried Celery Leaves or Parsley

Thoroughly dry all celery leaves or parsley in a cool oven or on the warming shelf. Pulverize by rubbing through a sieve and put in bottles. These make an unexcelled seasoning for soups.

Macédoine Garnish

A few spoonfuls of cooked peas, asparagus tips, carrots, or string-beans that have been served without a cream sauce, may any or all be reheated and used to garnish a platter of broiled chops. A few left-over radishes kept crisp and sliced very thin,

THE COOK BOOK OF LEFT-OVERS

without peeling, make an attractive garnish with parsley and slices of lemon for baked fish.

Purée of Vegetable

Take one creamed onion, a few peas, carrots, string-beans, or other green vegetables left from dinner, and while still slightly warm pass them through a sieve together. Keep in a cool place. Use this pulp the next day for a cream soup by seasoning it as needed, adding to it equal quantity white sauce No. 1 (see page 67, and heating all together. A spoonful or two of sweet cream is always an addition to such soups.

Vegetable Hash

Chop turnips, cabbage, beets, carrots, and onions, one or all, with cold boiled potatoes; season, moisten with little milk or gravy, and brown quickly in hot bacon fat, butter, or dripping.

Omelet with Vegetables

A breakfast omelet may be varied by spreading it, just before folding, with a few green peas or asparagus tips, or a little stewed corn or tomatoes that have been heated and well seasoned.

Asparagus with Cheese

2 cups cooked asparagus, cut in half-inch pieces	½ cup grated cheese
	4 tablespoonfuls melted butter
1 cup soft bread-crumbs	½ cup milk
	Salt, pepper

Moisten the bread-crumbs with the melted butter. Arrange in a baking-dish alternate layers of

VEGETABLES

bread-crumbs, asparagus and cheese, seasoning each layer. Sprinkle a few buttered cracker-crumbs on top. Pour the milk over all. Brown lightly in a hot oven.

Asparagus Soup

Cut the tender tips from cooked asparagus, set them aside and cook the stalks in some of the water in which the asparagus was cooked the day before. Cook down to a cupful, strain, and add to two cupfuls of white sauce No 1 A (see page 68). Heat to boiling, add the asparagus tips, and serve.

Baked-Bean and Tomato Purée

2 cups baked beans	1 onion, sliced
2 cups cold water	1 pint stewed and
1 tablespoonful flour	strained tomato
Sugar, salt, and pepper to taste	

Cook beans and onion in water until very soft. Strain. To one cup of thick bean pulp add tomato and seasoning. Thicken with the flour mixed smooth in two tablespoonfuls of water. Boil well after adding flour. If too thick, hot water may be added.

Baked-Bean Soup (with Milk)

1 cup bean pulp	2 cups thin white
Salt and pepper	sauce No. 1 (see page 67)

Prepare bean pulp as in preceding rule, combine it with the thin white sauce, add seasoning and, if necessary, hot milk to thin it.

THE COOK BOOK OF LEFT-OVERS

Baked-Bean Salad

Drain the liquid from baked beans, season more highly, and add a little chopped cucumber pickle. Serve in a bed of lettuce-leaves, dressing with mayonnaise. This salad may be the principal dish for a winter luncheon, as it has much food value.

A Good Way to Warm Over Baked Beans

Put into a hot frying-pan some of the pork cooked with the beans. When the fat has melted and is hot, pour in the beans, cover, and set pan back on stove where beans will cook slowly and brown underneath. Fold over like an omelet, turn out on a hot platter and serve with savory tomato sauce (see page 71), or tomato catsup. Garnish dish with parsley.

Baked-Bean Rarebit

1 cup grated cheese
1 cup milk
1 cup baked beans, mashed
Slices of Boston brown bread toast
1 tablespoonful butter
1 egg slightly beaten
A little salt and mixed mustard

Have the toast ready and hot. Cook in a saucepan, or chafing-dish over hot water. Melt the cheese in the hot butter. Add the seasoning and then the milk gradually, stirring until perfectly smooth. Then add the mashed beans and slightly beaten egg. Pour at once over the hot toast.

Succotash

Mix one cup of left-over beans, either shelled or string beans, with one cup of stewed corn, fresh

VEGETABLES

or canned. Season as needed, and heat slowly together. A little chopped cooked bacon may be added if desired.

Creamed Beets

Any left-over beets that have been served with butter and no vinegar may be creamed by way of variety. Chop them coarse, and to each cup of beets allow one cup of white sauce No. 2 (see page 68). Heat together.

Cabbage Scallop

Season more highly any left-over cooked cabbage, mix with white sauce No. 1 A (see page 68) in the proportion of one cup of sauce to two of cabbage. Butter a baking-dish, put in the mixture, and cover with buttered crumbs, using one tablespoonful melted butter to one-third cup of dried and rolled bread-crumbs. Bake in a quick oven until the sauce bubbles through the crumbs and they are brown. Individual ramekins may be used instead of the larger dish.

Creamed Cabbage in Cheese Shells

See page 169.

Carrots and Peas in Croustades

Prepare four croustades (for receipt, see below). Combine any left-over cooked carrots and peas, cutting the carrots into dice. Add seasoning if necessary, and mix with white sauce No. 2 (see page 68). Heat and serve in hot croustades.

Croustades

Cut two-inch slices of bread and trim off the crusts. Remove center a half inch from each edge, being careful not to break through the bottom. They may be either toasted, sautéd, buttered and browned in the oven, or fried in deep fat.

Carrot Croquettes

1 cup cooked carrots
1 cup cooked peas
1 cup white sauce No. 4 (see page 68)
1 egg
Salt, pepper, and grating of nutmeg

Press the carrots and peas through a purée sieve. They go through more easily if warm. Add seasoning, unbeaten egg, and white sauce, and set away to chill. Form into croquettes, roll in crumbs and egg, and fry in deep fat.

Cauliflower in Ramekins

Separate the flowerets of any cold cauliflower, toss them carefully about in a little melted butter, and pour over them an equal quantity of cheese sauce (see page 69). Place the mixture in ramekins, sprinkle the top lightly with buttered crumbs, and heat in oven until sauce bubbles through.

Sautéd Cauliflower

Cut cold cooked cauliflower into pieces of suitable size, dip lightly in flour seasoned with salt and pepper, and brown in hot bacon fat or dripping.

Celery Soup

Take the tough stalks, leaves, and roots of any celery. Wash carefully, cut in small pieces, cover

VEGETABLES

with about three cups of slightly salted boiling water, and cook until very soft. Pass all through a wire sieve. There should be two cups of pulp and liquid. Scald two cups of milk in a double boiler with one slice of onion. Strain and use this in making two cups white sauce No. 1 (see page 67). Add the celery mixture to this, and heat all together, but do not boil. Serve very hot with croutons (see page 149).

Celery Toast

Take the outer and less tender stalks of celery that are often thrown away, cut them into half-inch pieces, and cook in very slightly salted water until tender. Drain and use one-half cup of this water and one-half cup of milk to make a white sauce No. 2 (see page 68). Add the celery to the sauce, and pour over slices of nicely browned and buttered toast. Serve very hot.

Escalloped Celery

Use the coarse, large pieces of celery not suitable to serve uncooked. Cut them into small pieces. Butter a baking-dish, put in a layer of celery, then a layer of tomatoes (canned ones may be used). Sprinkle over them a teaspoonful of chopped onion, a little salt and pepper. Repeat, having last layer tomatoes. Cover with small cubes of bread and dot with a tablespoonful of butter. Bake in hot oven half an hour.

Corn "Oysters"

Grate the pulp from ears of any cooked sweet corn, and to each cup allow one egg beaten light, one tablespoonful milk, one tablespoonful flour, one teaspoonful melted butter, one half teaspoonful salt. Mix all together and drop by spoonfuls on a hot buttered griddle and brown on both sides. A little uncooked corn pulp is a great addition to these cakes.

Corn in Tomato Cases

Remove most of the pulp from six medium-sized tomatoes. Rub the inside of the cases with salt, pepper, and a little softened butter. Fill them with one cup of stewed corn mixed with one tablespoonful of grated cheese. Cover lightly with buttered crumbs, place in an agate pan, and bake until the cases are tender but not broken.

Corn Cakes

Take equal parts of mashed potato and cooked corn, add pepper, salt, and beaten egg to bind together. Dip the flat cakes in flour and sauté in hot butter or bacon fat, or form into balls, roll in bread-crumbs, in egg, and in crumbs again. Fry in deep fat. A tomato sauce may be served with these (see page 71).

Corn Soup

3 ears cooked corn	2 cups white sauce No. 1 (see page 67)
3 cups cold water	
Slice of onion	
1 egg	½ teaspoonful salt
A little celery or celery salt	

Score the corn by cutting with a sharp knife down each row of kernels. Scrape out the corn with a spoon, leaving hulls on the cob. Set the

VEGETABLES

scraped corn aside; there should be half a cupful. Cook cobs in water with onion, celery, and salt for half an hour, or until the water is reduced to one cupful. Add this to the white sauce, season more highly if necessary, boil up well, and when ready to serve put in the half cupful of corn. Heat a little, but do not boil. Beat egg and put into the tureen, pour the soup gradually over it, stirring, to mix evenly.

Baked Corn

1 cup cooked corn cut from cob
1 beaten egg
1 cup milk
1 chopped green pepper
Salt and pepper
Buttered bread-crumbs

Cut down rows of kernels with sharp knife and scrape out corn. Mix with egg, milk, salt, pepper, and chopped green pepper (being careful not to put in the seeds). Sprinkle top with crumbs and brown. Serve very hot. (It is cooked in about twenty minutes.)

Corn Pudding (from Uncooked Corn)

Corn on the cob loses flavor sooner than any vegetable. Do not try to serve it in that way unless perfectly fresh. If any uncooked ears are left over grate them. Six good-sized ears will give one and one-half cups of corn pulp. Add to this one egg beaten very light, one-quarter teaspoonful of salt, one teaspoonful of sugar, one teaspoonful of butter, and one-quarter cup of milk. Butter a quart baking-dish, pour in the mixture, and bake until firm in the center—about twenty-five minutes. Serve at once as a vegetable.

Stewed Cucumbers

Use those which are too large and old to slice raw. Pare them and cook in boiling salted water until tender. Slice in quarters lengthwise, and reheat in drawn butter sauce (see page 70) or white sauce No. 2 (see page 68). A dish similar to English vegetable marrow.

Scallop of Eggplant

Chop the remnants of fried eggplant rather coarse. Arrange in ramekins in alternate layers with well-buttered cracker-crumbs, finishing with the crumbs. Pour enough milk over so that it can just be seen, and brown in a hot oven. This dish resembles oysters in taste.

Cream-of-Lettuce Soup

1 qt. milk, scalded	3 white onions (cooked ones may be used)
1 pt. cold water	
Lettuce leaves	
2 or 3 small carrots	Flour for thickening (about 2½ tablespoonfuls)
Salt and pepper	
Handful of parsley	

When using the hearts of cabbage-lettuce for salad, prepare soup from the best outside leaves. Wash well lettuce leaves and parsley, add onions and carrots, pour over them the water and cook until the vegetables are soft enough to put through a strainer. (The pulp should be scraped from strainer and used.) Thicken this liquid with blended flour and water, let boil, then gradually add scalded milk.

VEGETABLES

Baked Macaroni

Chop two hard-cooked eggs rather coarse, season with pepper and salt, and mix lightly with two cups of cooked macaroni. Put in a buttered baking-dish and half fill with milk. Cover with buttered crumbs, place thin strips of bacon on top, and bake until the bacon is crisp.

Savory Macaroni

Crisp a little chopped bacon in a frying-pan, add a medium-sized onion sliced, and brown delicately. Toss up with this two cups of cold macaroni or macaroni and cheese until well mixed. Cover and set where it will warm through slowly.

Macaroni with Smoked Beef

Cook a little smoked beef in one tablespoonful of hot butter two or three minutes, add one-half tablespoonful of flour and a cup of milk, and stir often until it thickens. Add to this one and one-half cups of cold macaroni. Cook together until well heated. Serve on well-buttered hot toast.

Macaroni in Cheese Shells

See Cheese Shells with Creamed Cabbage, page 169.

Macaroni in Tomato Cases

Prepare several large tomatoes, cutting a slice off top and scraping out the inside pulp. Season the cases with salt and pepper, and fill with cooked macaroni. Over the top sprinkle buttered crumbs. Bake in a hot oven until the crumbs are brown and the tomatoes are partially cooked, but not long enough for them to lose their shape. The tomato pulp may be used for making soup or sauce.

Scallop of Onion and Potato

½ cup cold creamed onions
1½ cups cold potatoes
½ cup milk
1 tablespoonful butter
Salt and pepper

Butter a baking-dish. Slice half of the potatoes and season. Add the creamed onions. Cover with the rest of the potatoes, moisten with the milk, and dot with bits of butter. Bake one-half hour.

Parsnip Cakes

Use left-over boiled, buttered parsnips for making these cakes. Mash and season with salt and pepper, make into flat, round cakes, dip in flour, and sauté in hot melted beef-dripping or butter. Use just enough fat to keep the cakes from sticking to the pan, as they must not be greasy.

Green-Pea or Lima-Bean Soup

Cook any left-over peas or Lima beans with a little cold water until soft. Strain, and for every cup of the purée use two cups of white sauce No. 1 (see page 67). Combine mixtures, thinning with hot milk if necessary. Serve with croutons (see page 149). Dried Lima beans may be used.

Chopped Potatoes

Chop cold boiled potatoes fine and season well with salt and pepper. Heat a pan and melt in it one or two tablespoonfuls bacon fat or dripping.

VEGETABLES

When the fat is hot turn in the potatoes, smoothing them evenly in the pan. Cover with a tin, let them steam a few minutes, set on one side of the stove, and brown slowly. Turn over like an omelet and serve on hot platter. Stewed potatoes may be warmed over in this way, but do not chop them.

Stewed Potatoes

Cut cold baked or boiled potatoes into dice, put into a stew-pan with salt, a tiny bit of onion minced fine, and milk enough to half cover the potatoes. Set on the back of the stove and stew slowly, stirring with a fork occasionally, until all the milk is taken up. Season with butter and pepper and serve.

Scallop of Baked Potatoes and Cheese

Peel the left-over potatoes as soon as the meal is over. When ready to use, season them well with salt, pepper, and melted butter. In a buttered baking-dish arrange alternate layers of potatoes, grated cheese, and white sauce No. 2 (see page 68), having sauce on top. Sprinkle very lightly with buttered crumbs and heat in oven.

Potato Salad

New potatoes make the best salad, and if they have been boiled with the jackets on so much the better. Cut them in neat dice shapes. Season well with salt and pepper. To two cups add one-half teaspoonful onion-juice, if liked; one tablespoonful very finely minced capers, two tablespoonfuls melted butter, and one tablespoonful lemon-juice. Toss all together carefully so as not

THE COOK BOOK OF LEFT-OVERS

to break the potatoes. Chill. When ready to serve cover with a cooked salad dressing (see page 75), and arrange on a bed of crisp, white lettuce leaves. Garnish with rings of the white of hard-cooked egg, and sift yolk on top.

Potato Pyramids

To one cup of well-seasoned mashed potatoes add one egg yolk. Beat until light. Take up by tablespoonfuls and form into pyramid shapes by pointing one end, and broadening the other as a base to stand on. Set them on a buttered tin, brush over with beaten egg, and when ready to serve, brown lightly in the oven. These make an attractive garnish for meat dishes. Mashed potatoes are more easily handled if shaped directly after a meal is over, while still slightly warm.

Potato Patties

1½ cups boiled potatoes (sliced)
2 tablespoonfuls grated cheese
3 tablespoonfuls thick meat gravy
1½ teaspoonfuls onion-juice
Salt and pepper

Mix all together, place in buttered ramekins and heat in oven.

Cream-of-Potato Soup

1 cup mashed potatoes
3 cups milk
Salt and white pepper
1 tablespoonful butter
1 tablespoonful flour
1 slice of onion

Heat the milk and onion together, but do not **boil**: pour over the cold mashed potato and press

VEGETABLES

through a purée strainer. Melt butter, stir in flour and let bubble, but not brown; cool slightly and add the milk mixture slowly, stirring constantly until thickened. Add the seasoning and serve very hot, sprinkling a few nicely browned croutons or a little grated cheese over each plate of soup.

Potato Balls

Form any well-seasoned mashed potatoes into balls the size of English walnuts. With a teaspoon press a hollow in the top of each ball. Fill the space with one teaspoonful finely minced ham. Brush the balls with egg beaten with a little milk or water. Place on a greased pan and brown in oven. These make a good garnish and relish for a platter of chops.

Creamed Potatoes

Cut cold boiled potatoes in rather thick slices. Season with salt and a little white pepper. Toss them lightly in a little melted butter, being careful not to break them. Barely cover with rich milk and add one teaspoonful of flour to each cup of milk used. Cover and cook very slowly until the mixture is well thickened and creamy. Just before serving add a little finely chopped parsley. By way of variety, these may be served in turnip cups, which are made by cutting a slice from the bottom of small white turnips, paring them, and cooking in salted water; when tender, scoop out the inside, leaving a wall half an inch thick.

Potato Croutons

To one cup of mashed potato add one egg yolk, and beat well together. Spread half an inch thick on a flat, buttered platter, and when quite cool cut in two-inch squares, then each square diagonally across, to form triangular pieces. When ready to use, brush over with milk and brown lightly in the oven or in a very little fat in the frying-pan. These make an attractive garnish for a platter of chops or a platter of fried fish, alternated with slices of lemon.

Irish Potato Cake

To one cup of mashed potatoes add a well-beaten egg, half a cup of flour, and half a teaspoonful of salt. Mix well, turn out on well-floured board, adding a little more flour for kneading, and form into a cake half an inch thick. Cut this cake into wedge-shaped pieces and brown on a hot griddle to a light color. Then cover with an inverted pan and cook on the back of the stove until it is crusty—about twenty minutes. It is to be eaten hot with butter.

Potatoes with Cheese

2 rounded tablespoonfuls crumbled cheese	1½ cups milk
	6 small cold potatoes, sliced
3 tablespoonfuls butter	1 chopped sweet bell-pepper
3 tablespoonfuls flour	English walnuts
Salt, paprika and Tabasco	

Melt butter in saucepan, add cheese. When cheese is partly melted put in flour and cook until smooth. Season and add milk slowly, stirring constantly until thoroughly blended. Butter a baking-

VEGETABLES

dish, put in a layer of potatoes, sprinkle with chopped pepper, alternating potatoes and pepper until dish is full. Pour over this the cheese sauce. Sprinkle with the chopped walnuts and bits of butter. Brown and serve hot. The Spanish call this dish potatoes *con queso*. It is a Spanish receipt.

Browned Sweet Potatoes

Cut any cold sweet potatoes into slices lengthwise. Season with a little salt, dip in melted butter, roll lightly in sugar, and brown in oven.

Sweet-Potato Croquettes

Put through a meat grinder, using the finest cutter, enough cold boiled sweet potatoes to make one and one-half cups. Add one tablespoonful melted butter, half a tablespoonful brown sugar, beaten yolk of one egg, salt, pepper, cinnamon, and mace to taste. Mix well together, make into small croquettes, roll in fine crumbs, in egg, and in crumbs again. Fry in deep fat.

Creamed Spinach in Carrot Cups

Chop any cold cooked spinach very fine. Moisten with cream or white sauce No. 2 (see page 68) and heat. Cut medium-sized carrots to form cups and then scrape. Cook in boiling salted water until tender. Fill with the creamed spinach and serve hot.

Spinach Croquettes (with Fish)

1 cup spinach
1 cup cold flaked fish
1 tablespoonful milk
1 tablespoonful watercress, chopped fine
½ cup grated bread-crumbs
1½ tablespoonfuls lemon-juice
Pepper and salt

Moisten spinach with milk. Add lemon-juice, cress, and seasoning to fish. Mix all together with bread-crumbs. Form into croquettes, roll in crumbs, then in beaten egg, then in crumbs. Fry in deep fat. Serve with egg sauce (see page 69). This quantity will make six.

Spinach with Baked Eggs

Form any cold, well-seasoned spinach into a neat border on rounds of buttered toast. A full tablespoonful will answer for each piece of toast. Break an egg in the center of each round, season, and sprinkle very lightly with buttered crumbs. Bake in oven until the eggs are "set."

Squash Pudding

1½ cups cooked and strained squash	2 eggs
½ teaspoonful cinnamon	½ teaspoonful salt
⅓ cup sugar	1½ cups milk
	Grated rind of half a lemon

Gradually add the milk to the strained squash, then the sugar, salt, seasoning, slightly beaten eggs, and grated lemon-peel. Pour into a buttered pudding-dish and bake in moderate oven until thickened like custard. Serve very cold.

Vegetable Salads

These may be made of almost all kinds of cold cooked vegetables, using them separately or in combination. Bits of meat or fish may be added, or a few chopped nuts, if at hand. Lettuce or

VEGETABLES

other salad leaves may or may not be used, as convenient. The materials should be carefully prepared, and the salad chilled before serving. A better flavor is given to many salads by mixing the materials with a French dressing a short time before the mayonnaise is added, which is usually just before the salad is ready for the table.

Various garnishes are used, as olives, beets fresh or pickled, capers, hard-cooked eggs, pickled eggs, buds and leaves of nasturtiums, pickles, etc. The salad-maker should be artistic as well as ingenious, for harmony in color is essential. Overcrowding should be avoided. If the salad be served on a platter, leave a wide margin.

Kidney-Bean Salad

Combine one cup of cooked kidney-beans with one cup of crisp, tender summer cabbage, shredded. Add one green sweet pepper, first removing the seeds and shredding it fine. Cover with French dressing No. 1 (see page 73), or mayonnaise dressing (see page 74) and serve at once.

Salad of Greens

Left-over spinach or greens of any kind may be molded in small cups and served cold with French or mayonnaise dressing. The little balls of cottage cheese (see page 179) are good with this.

Mixed Salad (Italian)

Put lettuce leaves into a deep bowl, add a little cauliflower, two or three sardines, and two large potatoes cut in pieces. Mix well together, add salt, vinegar, and oil, and garnish with hard-cooked eggs.

Potato Salad

See page 113.

Hot Potato Salad

- 2 cups cold potato cubes
- 2 tablespoonfuls bacon, cut fine
- 1 tablespoonful cider vinegar
- 1 tablespoonful Tarragon vinegar
- 2 tablespoonfuls cream
- 1 teaspoonful scraped onion
- Parsley

Cook bacon, add onion, then potatoes, vinegar, cream, and one full teaspoonful minced parsley. Heat through and serve. Garnish with sprigs of parsley. A little chopped cooked beet is an addition to this salad.

Rice, Beet, and Celery Salad

Use equal quantities of cooked rice and cooked beets cut into cubes, and as much celery (cut very fine) as will equal the quantity of rice and beets together. Season. Serve with cooked salad dressing (see page 75), and garnish with celery tips and leaves.

Bermuda-Onion and Orange Salad

For the individual salad use one slice of Bermuda onion and two of orange. Serve on lettuce leaves with French dressing.

Green Pea Salad

Drain all liquid from a cup and a half of well-seasoned left-over green peas and chill them. When ready to prepare the salad, mix with the peas

VEGETABLES

half a cup of young, tender carrot, grated raw, reserving a little to garnish the top. Cover with mayonnaise (see page 74), or cooked salad dressing (see page 75), and serve at once on crisp, white lettuce leaves.

Green-Pea Salad in Egg Cases

Cut three or four hard-cooked eggs lengthwise and remove the yolks neatly. Crumble them into rather large pieces, season with salt, paprika, and toss them lightly about in melted butter. Mix with a cup of well-seasoned cold peas. Sprinkle a little salt and white pepper on the whites, put a spoonful of the peas in each, and cover with mayonnaise (see page 74). Serve on crisp lettuce leaves.

Spinach Salad

By the addition of a few hard-cooked eggs a cup of left-over creamed spinach can be made into an attractive luncheon salad. The spinach must be chopped very fine and moistened with a little white sauce No. 4 (see page 68). Form into balls the size of walnuts. Set away to chill. When ready to serve, slice rather thick as many hard-cooked eggs as needed; season them with salt and paprika. Mix them with the spinach-balls and pour mayonnaise dressing over all. Serve on heart lettuce leaves.

Winter Salad

Lettuce leaves	Neufchâtel or cream cheese
Cooked carrots	
Salt and pepper	Mayonnaise dressing

THE COOK BOOK OF LEFT-OVERS

Chop carrots fine, season and sprinkle over lettuce; make cheese into balls, and add to salad. Serve with mayonnaise (see page 74).

Tomatoes Sautéd, with Sauce

6 large slices tomato
¼ cup flour
½ cup milk
1 tablespoonful butter
Salt and pepper

(Any left-over sliced raw tomatoes, if firm and solid, may be kept covered with cold water for use next day.)

Dry the slices of tomato if they have been in water, season with salt and pepper, and dredge both sides well with flour. Melt butter in pan; when hot put in tomato, browning well on one side before turning. When both sides are brown remove to a hot platter. Gradually add milk to flour and butter in the pan, stirring well. Pour this sauce around the tomatoes and serve.

Mock Bisque Soup

1 cup stewed tomatoes, strained
⅛ teaspoonful soda
1 teaspoonful sugar
Paprika
2 cups scalded milk
2 tablespoonfuls butter
2 tablespoonfuls flour
½ teaspoonful salt

Heat the tomatoes and add soda. Cook butter and flour together, add seasoning, and pour in gradually the hot tomato. Let this boil up. Take from intense heat, and when below the boiling-point add the hot milk slowly, stirring constantly. Season more highly if desired. After the addition of the milk the soup should be kept hot, but must

VEGETABLES

not boil. Serve with crisp crackers, croutons (see page 149), or dried bread.

Scalloped Tomatoes

To every cup of stewed tomatoes add half a teaspoonful of scraped onion and more seasoning if necessary. Season some dried and rolled breadcrumbs and mix part of them with melted butter in the proportion of two tablespoonfuls butter to half a cup of crumbs. Butter small ramekins or large dish, sprinkle a layer of seasoned crumbs on the bottom, pour in tomato, and spread buttered crumbs over the top. Dot over with more butter if desired. Bake in hot oven about thirty-five minutes, browning crumbs well on top. A mixture of bread and cracker crumbs may be used.

Tomatoes with Scrambled Eggs

A few spoonfuls of stewed tomato may be mixed with eggs and scrambled. Beat eggs slightly with a fork, season, and mix with tomato. Melt in hot omelet-pan half a tablespoonful of butter, pour in eggs and tomato, and cook lightly, holding pan away from the intense heat. Pour over prepared toast or crisp triscuit. A full tablespoonful of tomato for every two eggs is a good proportion, but more may be used.

Jellied Tomato Salad

1 tablespoonful gelatine	Seasonings
	Lettuce leaves
1½ cups strained stewed tomatoes	Mayonnaise dressing

Season stewed tomatoes more highly by cook-

THE COOK BOOK OF LEFT-OVERS

ing with them a bit of bay leaf, small slice onion, two cloves, one or two stalks celery, sprig of parsley, few peppercorns, or little paprika, and salt if necessary Add a little water. Boil ten minutes Soak gelatine in one-fourth cup cold water. When soft, dissolve with hot strained tomato. (If tomato is very acid, add one-eighth teaspoonful of soda.) Pour into small cups or molds wet with cold water. When tomato is stiffened turn out on lettuce leaves. Sprinkle with chopped celery and serve with mayonnaise. Half this quantity will make four small molds. Canned tomatoes may be used.

Tomato Salad (with Cereal and Fish)

Combine in sandwich fashion a thin slice of cold farina or cream of wheat, molded in small, round tins, with two slices raw tomato. Dispose sandwich on lettuce, place on each side a small sardine, and on top a spoonful of mayonnaise (see page 74).

Tomato Toast

Add a few bits of celery to a cup or two of cold stewed tomatoes, and cook them down until well thickened Prepare a platter of toast, and butter it Scald a cup of cream, but do not boil When all is ready add a very little soda to the tomatoes, then the cream, pour directly over the toast and serve.

Home-made Tomato Paste

When tomatoes are very plentiful, and the supply is greater than the immediate need, it is a good plan to make a paste, which will keep for some time in a

VEGETABLES

cool place. Wash and scald the tomatoes. Strain through a fine sieve, and boil until thick. Put in glass jars. This will be found very useful in flavoring soups and sauces.

Tomato and Cheese Toast

Left-over slices of raw tomatoes may be acceptably utilized by placing one slice each on nicely browned and buttered toast circles. Season well with salt, pepper, and bits of butter. Cover with grated cheese and heat in oven until cheese is melted.

Cream of Turnip and Potato Soup

¾ cup mashed potatoes
3 cups scalded milk
1 tablespoonful flour
1 tablespoonful butter
¼ cup mashed turnip, white or yellow
½ teaspoonful salt
Few grains paprika

Pour the scalded milk over the mashed potatoes and turnips and strain through a fine wire sieve. Melt the butter, stir in the flour, and cook until bubbling, then add the hot milk mixture and cook until smooth and thickened. Serve very hot with rye-bread croutons. If the soup is too thick a little more hot milk may be added.

MY OWN RECEIPTS

MY OWN RECEIPTS

MY OWN RECEIPTS

MY OWN RECEIPTS

MY OWN RECEIPTS

WHAT TO DO WITH LEFT-OVER CEREALS

Most cereals are improved by long, slow cooking. This is emphatically true of hominy, cornmeal, and oatmeal, any one of which may be reheated to advantage. It is wise, therefore, to plan always for a remainder when cooking them. They are a comparatively cheap food, and when so cooked as to yield their full nutritive value, they form an important part of the dietary. They lend themselves easily to many transformations, and so give variety to the daily menu.

Cornmeal Circles

Do not allow left-over cornmeal mush to get perfectly cold before molding it. Beat it well, so that it will be perfectly smooth, and pour it into baking-powder tins, or half an inch deep in a flat pan, first moistening the tin with cold water. When ready to use cut in circles half an inch thick. If molded in a flat sheet use a biscuit cutter. Roll in milk, then very lightly in flour. Heat a little butter or bacon fat on a baking-tin until it bubbles, lay the circles on this, and brown lightly in a *very* hot oven. These make a good garnish for a meat dish, or may be served with maple syrup for breakfast or lunch.

Cereal Molded with Fruit

Take cream of wheat or wheatena left from breakfast. If very stiff add a little milk or water and stir into it a few scalded cut-up dates or figs. Pour into bowl or mold and serve cold as a dessert with sugar and cream.

Cereal with Tomato Salad

See Tomato Salad, page 124.

Cereal in Griddle Cakes

See Sour-Milk Griddle Cakes, page 150.

Farina Sponge

Stir into two cups of cooked farina the stiffly beaten white of one egg and one teaspoonful vanilla. Mold and serve with cream and sugar or soft custard If farina has been cooked very stiff, add a little hot milk or water, blending well.

Farina with Baked Apples

Wash four or five good baking apples, and with a corer remove all seeds and cores. Place them on an agate baking-pan with a tablespoonful of water on the bottom. Fill the centers with any left-over farina or cream of wheat, and put a small piece of butter on top of each. Sprinkle sugar and a few drops of lemon-juice over all and bake in a moderate oven until apples are soft. Serve hot for breakfast or luncheon.

Farina Pancakes

1 cup sweet milk	1 cup cooked farina
1 cup flour	1 egg
2 teaspoonfuls baking-powder	½ teaspoonful salt

CEREALS

Beat the egg and farina together until light and smooth, and stir in the milk. Sift the flour and salt together and add to the farina mixture. When ready to bake the cakes, stir in the baking-powder and beat the batter vigorously. These cakes will be found much more digestible than those made entirely of raw flour.

Hominy and Cheese Souffle

1 cup cooked hominy	1 cup grated cheese
¼ cup hot milk	2 eggs
Grated rind of half a lemon	Salt, paprika

With a fork beat up the cold hominy and the hot milk until very smooth. Add seasonings and grated cheese Separate the eggs and beat the yolks until thick and light, and stir into the mixture. Then fold in the stiffly beaten whites, pour into a buttered baking-dish, and bake in a hot oven until firm in center—about twenty minutes. Serve at once. This may also be cooked satisfactorily in a chafing-dish.

Hominy Balls

1 cup cooked hominy 1 egg yolk
Slight grating nutmeg Salt as needed

Mix all well together and form into smooth balls the size of large English walnuts. If the hominy is very stiff it should be beaten up with two tablespoonfuls of hot milk before the other things are added. Roll the balls in sifted white breadcrumbs, then in slightly beaten egg-white, and again in crumbs. Brown lightly in deep, hot fat This amount will make six balls.

Hominy with Bacon

Mold two cups of cooked hominy in a low dish of suitable size, first rinsing the dish with cold water. When ready to use turn it out on a baking-dish that can be sent to the table. Cover the hominy with thin slices of bacon and cook in a very hot oven until the bacon is crisp. Pour off the superfluous fat, surround with a border of poached eggs, and serve at once.

Hominy Pudding

½ cup boiled hominy
1 cup milk
2 teaspoonfuls sugar
1 tablespoonful melted butter
½ teaspoonful salt
2 eggs

Break the hominy apart with a fork and add the milk gradually to it. Stir in the butter, salt, sugar, and beaten yolks of eggs. Then fold in the stiffly beaten whites. Bake in an earthen dish about twenty minutes. Serve as a vegetable with veal.

Hominy Griddle Cakes

See Wheatena Griddle Cakes, page 143.

Southern Corn Cakes

1 cup boiled hominy
1 tablespoonful butter
2 eggs
½ cup milk, warm, but not hot
½ teaspoonful salt
½ cup cornmeal

Add the warm milk to the hominy slowly, beating until the mixture is very smooth, then stir in the butter, salt, well-beaten eggs, and cornmeal. The batter should look like thick cream. If too thick add a little more milk, or if too thin a little

CEREALS

more cornmeal. Bake in *thin* sheets in well-buttered flat pans about twenty-five minutes Cut into suitable-sized pieces before serving.

Oatmeal Molded with Raisins

Cover three tablespoonfuls of good raisins with rapidly boiling water and let stand just long enough to swell out and soften. Remove the seeds and cut in two. Stir these into two cups of cooked oatmeal while still warm, being careful not to break the grains of oatmeal. Moisten any small cups or jelly-glasses with cold water, half fill with the mixture, and set away in a cold place. Serve with cream or rich milk.

Oatmeal Gruel

Boil two-thirds of a cup of well-cooked oatmeal in one cup of boiling water fifteen minutes, or until the grains are very soft. Add an equal amount of milk, a few grains of salt, and a grating of nutmeg. A little cream is an improvement. It may be served strained or unstrained, as desired.

Browned Oatmeal

Cut cold oatmeal into slices. Beat up one egg with four tablespoonfuls of milk, and dip the oatmeal in this. Heat a little bacon fat to bubbling in a frying-pan and carefully brown the slices in it.

Oatmeal Bread

1 cup cooked oatmeal	½ cup lukewarm milk
1 tablespoonful sugar	Scant ½ cup lukewarm water
1 tablespoonful butter	½ yeast-cake
1 teaspoonful salt	About 4 cups flour

or enough to make a stiff drop batter

Mix the oatmeal, sugar, salt, butter, and lukewarm milk together. Dissolve the yeast in the luke-warm water and add to the mixture. Stir in the flour gradually, beating it well. The amount of flour necessary will be determined by the softness of the oatmeal. Let rise. This will make one loaf.

Rice with Apples

Pare, quarter, and core three or four medium-sized, tart apples. Cook them carefully in a syrup made of one cup of sugar and one cup of boiling water and one slice of lemon, being careful to keep the apples whole. While they are cooking put from one to two cups of cold cooked rice in a double boiler. Add one tablespoonful of sugar and one tablespoonful sweet cream to each cup of rice, stirring them in lightly with a fork. Cover and let heat thoroughly. Pile the rice in the center of a glass dish and place the apples as a border around it. Pour the remaining syrup over all and garnish with a few candied cherries. This can be served cold if desired.

Rice with Bananas

Peel and scrape three well-ripened bananas and mash them with a fork to a smooth, creamy pulp, adding a very few drops of lemon-juice. Stir this lightly into one cup of cold cooked rice and serve with or without sweetened cream. This is a nutritious dish, and attractive to children. Bananas have a much better flavor if purchased a little green, and if each one is then wrapped carefully in waxed paper, put in a clean, covered box

CEREALS

with a little excelsior, and ripened in a dry, warm place.

Cheesed Rice
See pages 165-66.

Rice in Cheese Shells
See Creamed Cabbage in Cheese Shells, page 169.

Rice with Tomatoes No. 1

Add one tablespoonful of bacon fat to each cup of cold cooked rice used, and put a layer of it in the bottom of a baking-dish. Cover with slices of raw, peeled tomatoes, and season with salt, pepper, a few bits of crushed bacon, and a tablespoonful of shredded green sweet pepper. Repeat until the dish is filled, reserving a little rice to cover the top. Bake in hot oven until the tomatoes are tender, covering the dish for the first ten minutes.

Rice with Tomatoes No. 2

Season about a cup and a half of stewed tomatoes extra well, adding a little onion-juice if liked. They should be stewed down thick, and not watery. Use an equal amount of tomatoes and cold rice Arrange in layers in a baking-dish and sprinkle each layer of rice with grated cheese before adding the tomatoes. Finish with rice and cheese on top Heat in oven just long enough for the cheese to melt.

Rice Omelet

1 small cup cold rice 3 eggs
2 tablespoonfuls milk 4 tablespoonfuls currant jelly
1 tablespoonful butter
1 scant teaspoonful salt

Beat the eggs well without separating, add rice, milk, and salt, stirring them in lightly. Melt the butter in a smooth frying-pan, and when hot pour in the omelet. As it cooks, lift carefully from one side to let the uncooked part run under. When all is creamy, spread with the jelly and fold. Serve on a hot platter. This makes a good luncheon dish.

Rice Muffins

½ cup cooked rice
¼ cup sweet milk
4 tablespoonfuls melted butter
4 teaspoonfuls baking-powder
2 cups flour
3 tablespoonfuls sugar
1 egg
1 scant teaspoonful salt

Sift together the sugar, salt, baking-powder, and flour. Beat the egg light, stir in the rice and milk, and add the dry materials. Beat in the butter last. Pour into warm, greased muffin-pans and bake in a hot oven about twenty-five minutes.

Rice Soup with Vegetables

When boiling rice in a quantity of water, as many people prefer to do, do not throw the water away. Drain it into a saucepan, and add a few diced carrots, a bit of celery tops and green onion, a sprig of parsley, and any other tender greens at hand. Season with salt and a little white pepper. Cover and simmer gently until the vegetables are done. More water may be added as needed, also a spoonful or two of cooked peas, or string-beans cut in thin strips. This makes a savory and nutritious dish. Another use for such water is to

CEREALS

let simmer in it a cup of good breakfast hash with just enough vegetables added to give it flavor.

German Rice Pudding

2 cups cold boiled rice   ¼ teaspoonful vanilla
½ cup cream   1 cup apple sauce

Sweeten the cream as liked, add the vanilla and a very little salt, and whip it Mix this with the rice and place in a pudding-dish in alternate layers with the apple sauce, having rice on top. Serve cold.

Rice Pudding with Stewed Fruit

Take two cups of rice pudding that has become very stiff when cold, and mix with it a cup of stewed and chopped tart prunes. Pile it lightly in a glass dish and serve it with the prune-juice, sweetened and thickened with a little corn-starch Other fruits than prunes may be used.

Risotto

Cut a small white onion into pieces and cook in butter until golden brown Add two cups of cooked rice, one cup of chicken stock, soup or gravy, and cook until rice has taken up the liquid Sprinkle one or two full tablespoonfuls grated cheese into rice, add pepper, salt, piece of butter, and chopped giblets if they are at hand.

Rice Custard No. 1 (very simple)

Cook one cup of cold boiled rice and one-half cup of milk in double boiler until rice is very soft. Beat one egg light with one tablespoonful sugar and a sprinkling of salt. Pour hot rice and milk gradually over egg mixture, stirring well. Transfer to dish in which custard is to be served. Grate nutmeg over top. Serve very cold.

Rice Custard No. 2

Combine left-over soft custard with cooked rice, using at least twice as much custard as rice. If whites of eggs are at hand, beat up a meringue, using one tablespoonful powdered sugar to each stiffly beaten white. Add few drops vanilla. Pile on top of custard and garnish with bits of jelly.

Baked Rice Pudding

1 cup cooked rice	1 tablespoonful butter
1½ cups milk	2 tablespoonfuls sugar
2 eggs	Vanilla or nutmeg
½ teaspoonful salt	Seeded raisins

Reheat rice, add melted butter, beaten eggs mixed with milk, and all other ingredients except flavoring. Cook five minutes in double boiler, add flavoring, put into buttered pudding-dish and bake twenty minutes, or until custard is "set." Serve warm or cold, plain or with preserve or jelly.

To Freshen up Rice or Bread Puddings

Remove crust from yesterday's pudding and turn out into smaller dish. Add hot milk, and (to a bread pudding) fresh crumbs for top, dotted over with butter. Bake again. Rice pudding may be reheated with hot milk, or if to be served cold, covered with a meringue flavored with lemon-juice and browned.

CEREALS

Lincoln Pudding

Mix two cups of well-cooked rice with three-fourths of a cup of milk, three tablespoonfuls sugar, a little salt, and well-beaten yolks of two eggs. Turn into a buttered pudding-dish and bake half an hour. Beat whites of eggs until stiff, add gradually three tablespoonfuls powdered sugar and juice of half a lemon. Pile meringue on pudding and bake twelve minutes in slow oven.

Rice Griddle Cakes

1 cup cold boiled rice	1 tablespoonful melted butter
¼ cup milk	
1 teaspoonful baking-powder	1 teaspoonful sugar
	¼ teaspoonful salt
About ½ cup flour (amount may vary)	1 egg, well beaten

Steam the cooked rice until very soft in part of the milk, using one-fourth cup. Add remainder of milk and other ingredients, beating well. Bake on hot griddle. This amount will make a plateful.

Rice Pudding (with Corn-starch)

1 cup boiled rice	2 eggs
3 cups milk	2 tablespoonfuls corn-starch
½ cup sugar	
Flavoring	Little salt

Beat yolks of eggs and mix with rice, sugar, and salt. Mix corn-starch with a little of the milk. Heat remainder, stir blended corn-starch into it and let boil a few minutes, stirring constantly. Put into double boiler and stir rice mixture into it. Cook until it begins to thicken, remove from fire, add flavoring (lemon or vanilla), and pour into dish. Beat whites of eggs with two tablespoonfuls powdered sugar, spread over top, and place dish in oven to brown meringue.

Sweet Rice Croquettes

1 cup rice, cooked very soft	Yolk of 1 egg
2 teaspoonfuls melted butter	¼ teaspoonful salt
	Crumbs and eggs for "breading"
1 teaspoonful sugar	Grated nutmeg to taste
Jelly	

Mix butter, sugar, salt, nutmeg, and beaten yolk of egg with the rice, form into croquettes and place a bit of jelly in the center of each, closing it well in with rice. Roll in fine sifted bread or cracker-crumbs, then in egg (one tablespoonful of water beaten with the egg), and in crumbs again. Fry in deep fat. Serve with lemon sauce or powdered sugar and cream.

Lemon Sauce No. 1

½ cup white sugar	1 tablespoonful flour, blended in 2 tablespoonfuls cold water
1 egg	
Few grains salt	
½ cup boiling water	
Juice of ½ lemon	

Beat sugar and well-beaten egg together. Stir blended flour into boiling water, let boil up well, and pour it over the egg and sugar, beating with Dover egg-beater. Add the lemon.

CEREALS

Wheatena Griddle Cakes

2 cups cooked wheatena
2 eggs
½ teaspoonful salt
½ cup cold water
½ teaspoonful baking-powder
Flour

Thin the cereal with water, add well-beaten eggs, and about a half cup flour sifted together with baking-powder and salt. Bake a trial cake on griddle to determine exact amount of flour needed. Hominy may be used instead of, or in combination with, wheatena.

Cereal Muffins

1½ cups flour
3 teaspoonfuls baking-powder
½ cup wheatena or other cereal
¾ cup milk
1 egg
1 tablespoonful butter
1 tablespoonful sugar
½ teaspoonful salt

Sift flour, measure it, and sift again with baking-powder, salt, and sugar. Break up the wheatena and thin carefully with milk; beat egg and add to it, stirring all into the dry materials. Add the butter melted, and put into buttered muffin-tins. Bake in quick oven from twenty to thirty minutes. Other cereals may be used in the same proportion.

MY OWN RECEIPTS

Wheaten Griddle Cakes

1 lb cooked wheat | ½ cup cold water
2 eggs | ½ teaspoonful baking
½ tsp cold milk | powder
 | ½ teaspoonful of Flour

Put the cooked wheat, a well beaten egg, and about ½ milk cup, Flour salted together, tablespoon, ... oil to taste ... hot cake griddle. Turn them once in a layer of fresh cooked. They may be eaten hot or cold, or as a pudding with...
... with cream.

Cereal Muffins

1 cup flour | 1 cup milk
1 teaspoonful baking | 1 egg
 powder | 1 tablespoon butter
1 cup cooked ... | 1 tablespoonful sugar
½ teaspoon salt | ½ teaspoonful salt

Sift flour and baking ... and stir together well, add ... and sugar. Place in the mixture ... and stir slowly with soft dough, ... mix, ... in stir ... into the dry mixture. Add the butter melted, and stir into batter, put in hot buttered ... and bake from twenty to twenty-five minutes. Gem molds may be used if not sound greased.

1914

MY OWN RECEIPTS

My OWN RECEIPTS

MY OWN RECEIPTS

MY OWN RECEIPTS

WHAT TO DO WITH LEFT-OVER BREAD

The uses for stale bread are so many and varied that it is obviously unwise to waste a particle. The bread-box requires constant supervision and care, especially in summer, when mold forms so quickly. It should be examined daily in hot weather, and in all seasons scalded and aired well before each fresh baking of bread. Small bits of bread should be slowly dried in the oven until crisp and brittle, then ground in the meat-chopper or rolled, and kept on hand in a glass jar for breading articles to be fried, for scallops, croquettes, dry stuffings, etc. The larger dried pieces, if cut into presentable shapes, are an excellent substitute for crackers or croutons with soup, and are often preferred to fresh bread. Small pieces and broken slices of stale bread may be used for moist stuffings for meat and poultry, for griddle-cakes, steamed bread, bread omelet, toast points, puddings of different sorts, and for other uses which will readily suggest themselves.

Croutons

Cut stale slices of bread half an inch thick. Trim off crusts (which may be set aside and used for puddings), butter the slices, and cut into half-inch cubes. Place on shallow pan and brown in a hot oven, turning them so that they may not burn. Serve with soup.

Steamed Bread

The very dry, hard pieces may be used in this way: Heat a griddle hot, butter it well, dip the pieces of bread *quickly* into hot salted water, and brown on both sides on the griddle. Eat with butter or with syrup.

To Freshen Dry Rolls or a Loaf of Dry Bread

Dip them quickly into *cold* water, drain, and heat in oven.

Bread Griddle-cakes (with Sour Milk)

Use equal quantities of sour milk and small, broken pieces of bread. Mix and let stand, covered, over one or two nights. Bits of rice may be added to this mixture if desired. In warm weather a little salt may be put with it. (In this case omit adding salt later.) When ready to use, put through colander. For each pint of mixture use one egg, one teaspoonful soda, one teaspoonful sugar, one-fourth teaspoonful salt, and about three-quarters of a cup sifted flour. It is always wise to bake a small cake first, that any lack in ingredients may be remedied at once. An extra yolk or small amount of uncooked egg may be added if at hand. Bake on hot griddle and serve with syrup.

Syrup

3½ cups light-brown sugar   2 cups cold water

BREAD

Cook sugar and water together, stirring until sugar is melted. Skim well while boiling. Boil for about thirty minutes, or until a little of the liquid put on cold saucer will thicken. Syrup may be flavored with maple, using part maple sugar.

Brewis (from Boston Brown Bread)

Take dry Boston brown bread and break into small pieces, having two cupfuls. Put into saucepan, add milk enough to cover (one pint or more). Let soak awhile on back of stove; when all is soft draw saucepan forward and let simmer until milk is absorbed. Add a little salt and a tablespoonful of butter. Serve with cream.

Boston-Brown-Bread Toast

Dry slightly in the oven the needed number of slices of brown bread and toast them carefully over a slow fire. Lay them on a warm platter, butter, and pour over them white sauce No. 1 (see page 67), to which one or two spoonfuls of finely chopped cooked ham have been added. Serve very hot.

Brown-Bread Relish

Put a little bacon fat in a frying-pan. When it is hot add any cut slices of Boston brown bread and brown carefully. Slip a poached egg on each slice and serve hot.

Bird's-nest Toast (for an Invalid)

Cut a slice of stale bread in a large circle. Toast it carefully over a slow fire until a delicate brown. Dip the edges very quickly in hot salted water and put it on a hot baking-tin, where it will keep warm.

Butter it if butter is allowed. Separate a perfectly fresh egg. Add a little salt to the white and beat to a stiff froth. Pile this on the toast, make a depression in the center, into which carefully slip the yolk. Heat in the oven just enough to "set" the yolk, and serve it on a warm plate.

Soft Buttered Toast

Toast six or eight slices of stale bread. Melt one-fourth cup butter in half a cup of boiling water in a bowl. Quickly dip each slice of toast in it, place in hot dish, and pour remainder of "dip" over all.

Milk Toast

Toast bread to a golden brown, having it *dry* all through. Keep hot in deep dish in oven. Make white sauce No. 1 (see page 67), using one and a half cups for six slices of toast. Pour between and over slices of toast and serve hot. If a softer toast is liked, quickly dip slices in hot water or milk before adding sauce.

Bread Sticks

Remove the crusts from any slices of stale, close-textured bread, and cut in strips about five inches long and one-half inch wide. Roll in melted butter and brown delicately in the oven, or fry in deep hot fat without rolling in butter. These can be served with cheese instead of crackers.

Quick Bread Omelet

3 eggs	5 tablespoonfuls white sauce No. 1 (see page 67)
½ cup soft bread-crumbs	
Dash of cayenne	Salt and pepper

Make the white sauce and pour while hot over bread-crumbs, mixing and mashing them well. Beat yolks of eggs until thick, and stir them, with the extra seasoning, into the white sauce mixture. Cut and fold in the stiffly beaten whites. Have ready a hot, buttered frying-pan, turn in omelet, and cook lightly. Set pan in oven to dry off top of omelet, turn out on warm platter, and serve at once.

Bread Sauce

Cook in double boiler half a pint of milk with a small onion and two cloves. Strain, put in saucepan, and add half a cup grated white bread-crumbs from the inside of the loaf, mixed to a paste with some of the hot milk. Let boil a few minutes, stirring and blending well. Add one-fourth teaspoonful salt, a dash of cayenne, and a small piece of butter just before taking up. Serve with boiled fowl. Two teaspoonfuls chopped parsley may be added if desired.

Bread Cereal

Dry bread in oven until crisp and brown. Roll on board, or put through meat grinder, having crumbs coarse. Serve warm as a breakfast food with cream.

Crust Coffee

Cut the crusts from slices of Boston brown bread and brown in oven until they are much darker in color, but not burned. Put into saucepan, pour boiling water on them, and let stand covered where they will keep hot for fifteen minutes. Pour off the liquid into a hot coffee-pot, and serve with sugar and cream. An excellent and wholesome substitute for coffee.

Chocolate Bread Pudding

1 pint milk	Yolks 2 eggs
4 tablespoonfuls grated chocolate	1½ cups stale bread-crumbs (soaked in ⅔ cup water)
2 tablespoonfuls butter	2 tablespoonfuls powdered sugar
⅓ cup sugar	Vanilla
Whites 2 eggs	

Scald milk, add chocolate melted over hot water, butter, and sugar. Stir well and pour over the soft bread-crumbs and beaten yolks of eggs. Add one teaspoonful vanilla, pour into buttered pudding-dish, and bake half an hour. Make meringue of whites of eggs beaten until stiff and dry, the powdered sugar, and half a teaspoonful vanilla. It may be served warm or cold.

Bread Pudding

3 eggs	2 tablespoonfuls butter
2 cups bread-crumbs	1 quart milk
½ teaspoonful cinnamon	½ teaspoonful salt
½ cup raisins	Little nutmeg

Scald milk. Add butter and bread-crumbs. Beat eggs light and add with salt and spice to bread mixture. Bake lightly in moderate oven about an hour. To be served warm with hard sauce (page 158) or lemon sauce No. 2 (see below).

BREAD

Lemon Sauce No. 2

½ pint sugar
⅓ cup butter
1 egg
Juice of half a lemon
3 tablespoonfuls boiling water

Cream butter and sugar well, add egg, beaten very light, and lemon-juice. Beat all together thoroughly and add the boiling water, a tablespoonful at a time.

Mock Indian Pudding

Butter on both sides three slices of white bread, add one quart of milk, two-thirds of a cup of molasses, and a little salt. Bake slowly about two and a half hours, stirring often until well mixed. Serve with cream.

Brown Betty

Place alternate layers of chopped juicy apples and stale bread-crumbs in buttered baking-dish, having crumbs on bottom. Add cinnamon and sugar to each layer of apple, using more sugar if apples are very tart. The top layer to be bread-crumbs with more butter. Bake for an hour, covering dish at first. Brown crumbs on top. Serve warm with hard or liquid sauce, or, if preferred, sugar and cream. Scant sugar in pudding if sweet sauce is used.

Currant Pudding

1 pint currants
½ cup sugar
6 or 8 slices stale bread

Stew fruit, boiling about five minutes. Add sugar just before taking off fire. Cut crusts from bread and fit slices neatly into bowl or dish from which the pudding will turn out well. Pour currants between and over slices, covering all parts of bread. Cover closely, set away in cool place. Serve cold with cream and sugar.

Cherry Pudding

1 cup of fine sifted bread-crumbs	About ½ cup of milk or enough to make a soft dough
1 cup flour	½ teaspoonful salt
4 tablespoonfuls sugar	2 teaspoonfuls baking-powder
1 cup pitted cherries	1 egg
4 tablespoonfuls butter	

Mix crumbs, flour, sugar, salt, and baking-powder together. Rub in the butter with a spoon. Beat the egg until light, add the milk, and stir into the dry materials. Sprinkle the least bit of flour on the cherries and add them. Bake about half an hour. Serve hot with vanilla sauce.

Vanilla Sauce

1 cup boiling water	1 egg yolk
4 tablespoonfuls sugar	1 tablespoonful corn-starch
½ teaspoonful lemon-juice or a bit of lemon-rind	1 teaspoonful vanilla
A little salt	1 teaspoonful butter

Mix the corn-starch, sugar, and salt, and pour the boiling water over them. Cook until thickened. Remove from fire, beat in the egg yolk, butter, and flavoring.

BREAD

New England Pan Pie ("Pandowdy")

Apples	Pieces stale bread
Light bread dough	½ teaspoonful clove
½ cup molasses	½ teaspoonful cinnamon
½ cup sugar	
2 tablespoonfuls butter	¼ teaspoonful nutmeg

Fill a good-sized baking-dish with juicy apples pared and quartered, cover with a crust made of bread dough (or pastry, page 27), and bake until apples are soft and crust brown. Take off crust while adding to apples the butter, molasses, sugar, spice, and pieces of bread. (Amount of bread may vary.) Replace crust, having brown side down, and spread with some of the apple. Cover closely with a pan and bake in moderate oven two hours. Turn out on flat dish and serve cold with cream.

Spiced Graham Pudding

Take half a loaf of stale graham bread before it gets very dry, and cut off all the hard crust. Press seeded raisins well into the bread to cover the entire surface. Make a custard mixture of two cups of cold milk, two eggs, four tablespoonfuls of sugar, one-half teaspoonful of salt, one teaspoonful mixed spices, and one-quarter teaspoonful nutmeg Mix the sugar, salt, and spices together and add them to the beaten eggs. Pour in the milk. Soak the bread in this until it entirely absorbs it, turning occasionally so all sides are moistened. Put into a buttered pudding-mold or tightly covered pail, and steam one hour. Serve with maple sauce.

Maple Sauce

2 tablespoonfuls butter	½ cup soft brown sugar
A few drops lemon-juice	Scant ¼ teaspoonful maple extract

Cream the butter, add the sugar slowly, and beat well. Then stir in the flavoring. Set in a cool place to harden a little before using.

Steamed Bread Pudding

1 pint bread-crumbs	1 egg, well beaten
1 cup cold water	1 cup flour
1 cup molasses	1 teaspoonful cinnamon
1 teaspoonful soda, dissolved in hot water	1 teaspoonful clove
	1 cup raisins, cleaned
½ teaspoonful salt	

Mix together and steam three hours. If half rule is used, do not divide the egg. Nuts may be substituted for part of raisins if desired. Serve with hard sauce.

Hard Sauce

⅓ cup butter	½ teaspoonful vanilla
1 cup sifted powdered sugar	Nutmeg.

Cream butter, add gradually powdered sugar, and beat together until light. Add vanilla, pile in dish in which it is to be served, grate nutmeg over top, and set in ice-box until needed.

Toast Pudding

Cut five or six slices of light, stale bread half an inch thick. Mix one beaten egg with one cup milk, add one-fourth teaspoonful salt, and soak bread

BREAD

in this for fifteen minutes. Brown in hot butter in a frying-pan or griddle. Serve with raisin sauce.

Raisin Sauce

1½ cups water	1 teaspoonful flour
⅓ cup raisins	Sprinkling of salt
¼ cup brown or white sugar	Nutmeg
	1 teaspoonful butter

Boil raisins in water for fifteen minutes, add sugar, boil fifteen minutes longer. Thicken with the flour blended with small amount of water. Add salt and spice, and just before taking up, the butter. Stir well and serve.

Cream Puffs (from Pop-overs)

Take any pop-overs left from breakfast and make an opening in them just large enough to neatly fill the center. For four to six pop-overs make a filling of one-half cup of cream sweetened with two tablespoonfuls of sugar and flavored with one-quarter teaspoonful of vanilla or a little lemon-juice Add a very little salt and whip it. Stir in one teaspoonful of melted gelatine. Set on the ice to chill. When ready to serve stir in half a cup of any fresh fruit that has been sugared, then drain off the juice, and fill the pop-overs. Serve at once. The fruit may be omitted.

Vegetarian Loaf

2 cups white bread-crumbs	2 beaten eggs
	½ teaspoonful salt
1 cup milk	1 teaspoonful poultry dressing
2 cups pecan nuts or English walnuts	½ cup melted butter
Pepper and celery salt	

THE COOK BOOK OF LEFT-OVERS

Soak bread-crumbs in milk and eggs. Put nuts through meat grinder, but do not use finest cutter, as they should not be as fine as meal. Mix with crumbs, milk, eggs, and seasoning. Grease oblong bread-pan and put in mixture, pouring a little melted butter over top. Bake half an hour, basting often with butter. Turn out on platter and serve hot, or slice cold. Use parsley for garnish.

MY OWN RECEIPTS

MY OWN RECEIPTS

MY OWN RECEIPTS

MY OWN RECEIPTS

WHAT TO DO WITH BITS OF CHEESE

Cheese is an excellent accompaniment to many made-over dishes, particularly to starchy foods and those lacking fat, as it adds both flavor and food value. Being a concentrated food, a little of it goes a long way, so there is no excuse for the least particle being wasted. When cheese comes from the store it should be wrapped in a clean cloth and kept in a cool, dry place. If the cloth is moistened with vinegar this will retard the formation of mold Grate all the little dry pieces as they accumulate, and put in a covered glass jar. It is well to keep a jar or two of Parmesan cheese, which comes grated, always on hand to help out. Care must be taken not to overcook cheese, as this renders it indigestible. When it is to be added to a hot mixture let this be done, whenever possible, just before taking from the fire.

Cheesed Rice No. 1

Put in a double boiler or chafing-dish two cups of cold boiled rice and a scant half cup of hot milk, and heat thoroughly over water. Then sprinkle lightly over it half a cup of grated cheese and a few shreds of pimento. Cover tightly and let stand over the hot water until the cheese is melted. This is acceptable for Sunday tea.

Cheesed Rice No. 2

Take half a cup of rice. Take any odds and ends of dry cheese too small to grate and melt them in the oven, seasoning with salt, pepper, and a little mixed mustard. Turn the rice out on a hot platter, place three or four poached eggs on top, and pour the melted cheese over.

Cheese with Creamed Sprouts

Make a cup of white sauce No. 2 (see page 68), and add one cup of left-over Brussels sprouts to the hot sauce, being careful not to break them. When well heated add half a cup of grated cheese and remove from the fire as soon as the cheese is melted. Serve on squares of well-buttered toast.

Tomato Rarebit

½ cup stewed tomatoes   1 tablespoonful butter
½ cup grated cheese   1 egg
Salt and cayenne as needed

Strain out the seeds from the cup of well-seasoned stewed tomatoes, pressing through all of the pulp, and let simmer uncovered until reduced to half a cup. Cook this rarebit over water, either in a double boiler or chafing-dish. Melt the butter and add the cheese, and stir until the cheese melts. Add seasonings and tomato pulp and heat together, stirring constantly. Blend a little of this hot mixture with the beaten egg before adding it. Remove from the heat as soon as the egg is

CHEESE

well stirred in, and serve on slices of crisp ryebread toast.

Cheese Dreams

With a biscuit cutter cut circles from very thin slices of any kind of close-textured bread. Lay very thinly shaved slices of cheese between the bread to form sandwiches. Brown lightly in hot butter in a frying-pan. Serve hot.

Cheese Canapes

With a biscuit cutter cut small circles from rather thin slices of rye bread, and brown them lightly in a little bacon fat. Put a few shreds of pimento on each circle, cover with grated cheese, and set in oven just long enough to melt the cheese. Serve hot as a first course.

Cheese Sandwiches (of Hot Biscuits)

Have ready some very thin slices of cheese. Bake a pan of biscuits (see Surprise Biscuits, page 12), and immediately on taking them from the oven break them open quickly, spread lightly with butter, and lay a slice of cheese between each. Cover with a warm napkin and serve promptly. It is necessary to work quickly so the warmth of the biscuit will melt the cheese. These are good for an emergency luncheon.

Cream-Cheese Salad

Mix an equal amount of cream cheese and chopped nuts well together. Add a little finely minced parsley. Form into balls the size of small English walnuts and set away to chill. When ready to serve the salad, dress a platter of crisp white lettuce leaves that have been well dried, with enough French dressing (see page 73) to moisten. Lay the cheese balls on the lettuce and serve at once. Cream cheese spoils very quickly, so any leftovers of it should be kept very cold and utilized within twenty-four hours.

Cream Cheese on Crisp Crackers

Take any unsweetened crackers. If they are not very crisp, put them on a flat baking tin and set in a moderate oven for a few minutes. Spread with beach-plum or Bar-le-Duc jelly, and drop a small teaspoonful of cream cheese in the center of each cracker.

Cheese Toast

Dry slightly in the oven and then toast as many slices of Boston brown bread as needed. Butter and keep them warm. Make enough white sauce No. 2 (see page 68) to well cover the toast, using paprika instead of pepper. When the sauce bubbles add one-half cup grated cheese to each cup of sauce, remove from the fire at once, and pour over the toast. Serve very hot.

Cheese Macaroons

Spread some macaroons lightly with any tart jelly at hand. Press two together with a layer of snappy cheese between.

German Pot-cheese Cake

1 cup butter	1 cup pot-cheese
1 cup sugar	1 cup grated bread-
3 eggs	crumbs
Grating of lemon-rind	½ teaspoonful vanilla
¼ teaspoonful salt	

CHEESE

Cream the butter and sugar well together. Separate the eggs, adding the yolks one at a time, then the flavoring, and beat the mixture until *very* light. Stir in the pot-cheese and grated bread-crumbs. Fold in the stiffly beaten whites. Bake in a moderate oven.

Cheese and Fish Soufflé

Cook half a cup of bread-crumbs to a paste in half a cup of rich milk, and stir in half a cup of mild cheese, grated. To the yolks of two eggs add a little mustard, salt, cayenne, few drops of Worcestershire, half a teaspoonful lemon-juice, a little minced parsley, and half a cup of cooked fish, flaked. Add to first mixture and let cool Fold in the stiffly beaten whites of two eggs. Set in a pan of hot water and bake about twenty-five minutes.

Cheese Shell Filled with Creamed Cabbage

A small head of young cabbage should be boiled in salted water until tender. Drain, chop, and season it. There should be two cups. Put it in an empty Edam or pineapple cheese shell in alternate layers with one cup of white sauce No. 2 (see page 68). Heat in the oven until the sauce bubbles. This will give the cabbage a delicate cheese flavor. Boiled macaroni or rice may also be reheated in cheese shells to advantage.

Cheese Sticks (from Pie Crust)

When there is not enough crust for another pie, roll[1] it thin, cut in strips about three inches long and one inch wide. Moisten the edges and spread

THE COOK BOOK OF LEFT-OVERS

with a little snappy cheese. Roll up and press the outer edge well down. Brown lightly in the oven.

Cheese Balls

To cream cheese add a dash of Tabasco, a pinch of salt, enough paprika to give it a pink color, and cream to make a paste. Form into small balls and roll in finely chopped black walnuts. Serve with lettuce and French dressing.

Cheese and Green Peppers

To soft cheese such as is packed in jars add desired amount of chopped green peppers. Use for sandwiches or serve from dish.

Cheese Soufflé

1 cup white sauce No. 3 (see page 68)
¼ teaspoonful salt
½ cup grated cheese
3 egg whites
3 egg yolks
Dash of cayenne

Make white sauce; while hot add cheese, salt, and cayenne, stirring as cheese melts. Remove from heat and add yolks of eggs already beaten until thick. Let cool, cut and fold in stiffly beaten whites of eggs, turn into buttered baking-dish holding a quart, and bake in moderate oven twenty to twenty-five minutes. Serve at once.

Cheese Soup

1½ cups milk
½ cup cooked diced carrots and carrot-juice
¼ teaspoonful salt
¼ cup grated cheese
1 egg
¼ teaspoonful ground mace
Little cayenne

CHEESE

Cook milk in double boiler with carrots, adding spice and seasoning. When the carrots are very soft, strain and press through a sieve, pouring liquid on to a beaten egg, stirring carefully meanwhile. Return the soup to the double boiler, reheat, add grated cheese, and serve when this is melted.

Welsh Rarebit

1 tablespoonful butter
$\frac{1}{4}$ cup cream
$\frac{1}{2}$ cup cheese, broken in small pieces
$\frac{1}{2}$ teaspoonful lemon-juice
$\frac{1}{2}$ teaspoonful Worcestershire sauce

1 egg, slightly beaten with 1 tablespoonful of water
$\frac{1}{8}$ teaspoonful mustard
$\frac{1}{4}$ teaspoonful celery salt
Toasted bread or crisp crackers
Dash of cayenne

Melt butter in double boiler, add cheese and cream, and while this is melting stir in mustard, celery salt, and cayenne previously mixed together. When the cheese mixture has begun to thicken and look creamy, carefully stir in the egg. Just before taking up add lemon-juice and Worcestershire. Serve at once on toast or crackers. Avoid overcooking, or the cheese will become stringy.

Mock Welsh Rarebit

3 tablespoonfuls butter
1 tablespoonful flour
1 well-beaten egg
$\frac{1}{2}$ cup cheese
$\frac{1}{2}$ cup cold water

$\frac{1}{2}$ cup milk
$\frac{1}{4}$ teaspoonful salt
$\frac{1}{2}$ cup white bread-crumbs
Toasted crackers
Cayenne

THE COOK BOOK OF LEFT-OVERS

Soak crumbs in water fifteen minutes. Prepare and measure all ingredients, as everything should be at hand before beginning to cook. Melt butter, add flour, and while cooking add cheese crumbled in small pieces. Cook and stir till smooth, and cheese is almost melted, then add milk gradually. The soft bread-crumbs and seasoning come next. When well blended, add the egg mixed with a tablespoonful cold water. Cook and stir carefully until slightly thickened, pour over hot crackers, and serve at once.

MY OWN RECEIPTS

MY OWN RECEIPTS

MY OWN RECEIPTS

MY OWN RECEIPTS

WHAT TO DO WITH SOUR MILK AND CREAM

It often happens in warm weather, with even a limited milk supply, that some of it gets sour before it can be used. This sour milk should never be wasted, even if there is only a little. It is a valuable kitchen asset. Have a clean glass or earthen receptacle to pour the remnants in, and keep in the ice-box or a cold place until enough has accumulated to make from a half to one cup. Then plan to use it as soon as it thickens, for milk becomes bitter if it stands too long.

In the following receipts all soda measurements should be level and exact.

Boston Brown Bread

1 cup corn-meal
1 cup Graham flour
⅓ cup molasses
1⅔ cups thick sour milk
1 teaspoonful soda
½ teaspoonful salt

Sift the meal and flour before measuring. Dissolve soda in little hot water, add to milk. Combine wet and dry materials, pour into greased mold (leaving room for bread to rise), cover with greased cover, and steam four hours. Take off cover and bake in oven half an hour. This will make one loaf.

Emergency Biscuits

2 cups flour	1 cup thick sour milk
1 tablespoonful shortening	¼ teaspoonful salt
	½ teaspoonful soda

Sift the flour, salt, and soda well together. Rub in the shortening with a spoon. Add the milk and stir lightly. The dough should be soft. Drop by spoonfuls into greased muffin-tins and bake in a hot oven about twenty minutes.

Sour-milk Griddle-cakes

1 cup thick sour milk	1 egg
½ cup any cooked cereal	About ¾ cup flour
	½ teaspoonful soda
⅛ teaspoonful salt	

Beat sour milk, cereal, and egg well together. Sift flour and salt and add them. When ready to bake the cakes add the soda and beat the batter vigorously. It should look like thick cream. If too thin add a little more flour, and if too thick add more sour milk or a little water.

Bread Griddle-cakes (with Sour Milk)

See page 150.

Breakfast Straws

1 cup of thick sour milk	½ teaspoonful cinnamon
½ cup dried currants	About 2 cups flour, and enough more to roll
½ teaspoonful soda	
¼ teaspoonful salt	

SOUR MILK AND CREAM

Sift the flour, soda, salt, and cinnamon together; add the currants. Stir in the milk quickly. The dough should be stiff enough to roll out. Cut into narrow strips and fry in hot fat. These are good with coffee.

Corn Bread

- 1 cup corn-meal (scant)
- ½ cup flour
- 1 egg, well beaten
- 1 cup thick sour milk
- ½ teaspoonful salt
- ½ teaspoonful soda
- 1 tablespoonful sugar
- 1 tablespoonful melted beef dripping or chicken fat

Dissolve soda in hot water, put with sour milk. Sift and mix dry materials; add egg, milk, and shortening. Bake in muffin-tins half an hour A little sour cream, if at hand, may be substituted for some of milk. In that case omit shortening.

Cottage Cheese No. 1

Cook one pint of thick sour milk in double boiler over simmering water until it begins to whey. Strain through fine napkin, squeeze out the whey, and add three teaspoonfuls of cream, a little salt, and white pepper. Make into small balls. This amount makes four or five.

Cottage Cheese No. 2

To three pints of thick sour milk add one pint of boiling or *very* hot water. Let stand half an hour, pour off water, and put curd in small bag to drain (a small salt-bag may be used). Add salt, a little soft butter, and cream if at hand.

Eggless Cookies (Plain)

- ½ cup butter (chicken fat or beef dripping may be substituted)
- 1 cup sugar
- 1 cup thick sour milk
- ¾ teaspoonful soda
- ½ teaspoonful cinnamon
- ½ teaspoonful clove
- Salt
- 2 cups flour; enough more to roll out

Cream butter and sugar. Dissolve soda in hot water and add to milk. Mix all together, making soft dough. Use as little extra flour as possible. Chill dough, and use only small portion at a time. Roll out thin, sprinkle a little granulated sugar and two or three currants on top. Bake in hot oven.

Graham Bread

- 1 cup thick sour milk
- ½ cup molasses
- 1 cup Graham flour
- ¼ teaspoonful salt
- 1 cup wheat flour
- ½ teaspoonful baking-powder
- 1 teaspoonful soda

Sift Graham and wheat flour and measure. Add baking-powder and salt; sift again. Dissolve soda in hot water, add to sour milk, and mix with molasses. Combine wet and dry mixtures, bake in bread-pan one and one-half hours. This will make one loaf.

Sour-milk Gingerbread

- 1 scant cup molasses
- ½ cup thick sour milk
- 4 tablespoonfuls melted shortening
- 2 cups flour
- 1 egg
- 4 tablespoonfuls cocoa
- 1 teaspoonful ginger
- ½ teaspoonful soda
- ⅛ teaspoonful salt

SOUR MILK AND CREAM

Mix molasses, sour milk, and beaten egg well together, and add cocoa, ginger, salt, and flour. Dissolve the soda in a very little hot water and add it. Beat in the melted shortening at the last. Bake in a shallow pan or muffin-tins in a moderate oven about twenty-five minutes. A mixture of Porto Rico and New Orleans molasses gives the best results.

Sour-Cream Filling for Cake

Sweeten and chill a cupful of sour cream. Whip it, keeping it cold while doing so, and when stiff fold in a cup of chopped nuts. This is excellent for layer cakes. If for any reason the cream does not become stiff, add one teaspoonful of melted gelatine at the last and set on the ice.

Cream Spice Cake

- 1 cup sour cream
- 1 cup sugar
- 1 egg, well beaten
- 1 teaspoonful soda
- 1 cup raisins, chopped and floured
- Sprinkling of salt (if needed)
- 2 cups bread flour
- $\frac{1}{2}$ teaspoonful vanilla
- 2 teaspoonfuls grated nutmeg
- 2 teaspoonfuls cinnamon
- 1 teaspoonful allspice
- $\frac{1}{2}$ teaspoonful clove

Mix all together, adding to sour cream the soda dissolved in a little hot water. Bake as a loaf for one hour, or in muffin-tins. A small amount of sour cream may always be set aside, and more added each day as it is left, until there is a cupful. When each addition is made, stir well, putting in a little salt, and it will keep some time.

THE COOK BOOK OF LEFT-OVERS

Cream Filling for Cake

Mix equal quantities of sour cream, chopped nuts and raisins. Add a little lemon-juice and powdered sugar.

MY OWN RECEIPTS

MY OWN RECEIPTS

MY OWN RECEIPTS

MY OWN RECEIPTS

WHAT TO DO WITH WHITES OR YOLKS OF EGGS

Eggs should always be wiped with a damp cloth before they are broken. The shells are then all ready to be used for clearing coffee, soup, or jelly. When any uncooked whites or yolks are left over put them in a cup, cover with a folded damp cloth, and slip a rubber band around it. Leftover poached or soft-cooked eggs may be carefully returned to hot water and cooked until hard, and then chopped and mixed with cold meat or fish dishes (see Kedjeree, page 89, and Fish with Pie Crust, page 94), or sliced and used for salads, (see Green Pea Salad in Egg Cases, page 121), etc. Bits of omelet or scrambled eggs are always permissible in a meat hash.

"Floating Island" for Soft Custard (Using up Whites of Eggs)

Beat up whites of eggs until stiff, gradually beat in very little powdered sugar, and drop large spoonfuls in hot (not boiling) milk in frying-pan. Dip milk over egg, that it may cook slightly. Take up in a skimmer and drain. Serve on sof custard with a bit of bright jelly on top of each spoonful.

Snow Pudding (to Use up Whites of Eggs)

Mix four tablespoonfuls of sugar with four tablespoonfuls of corn-starch and one-eighth teaspoonful of salt. Add a pint of boiling water and boil five minutes, stirring constantly. Put in double boiler and let cook half an hour. Cool and flavor as desired. Fold in the stiffly beaten whites of two or three eggs and a cup of any fresh or canned fruit, without juice, and mold it. Serve with sweetened cream.

Blanc Mange (to Use up Whites of Eggs)

1 pint milk (scalded)	1 tablespoonful sugar
5 tablespoonfuls corn-starch	Whites of 3 eggs
	Grated lemon-rind
⅛ teaspoonful salt	

Blend corn-starch with one-fourth cup cold milk, add to scalded milk, and cook in double boiler, then directly over fire a few minutes. Add other ingredients. Beat in stiffly beaten whites of eggs after corn-starch is taken from fire. Mold. Serve with sugar and cream.

White Cake (to Use up Whites of Eggs)

½ cup butter	2 cups bread flour
1 cup sugar	4 teaspoonfuls baking-powder
½ cup milk	
Few grains of salt	½ teaspoonful almond extract
Whites of 3 eggs	

Cream butter and sugar, add flour (with baking-powder and salt), and milk alternately. Flavor-

EGGS

ing and stiffly beaten whites of eggs added last. Line pan with paper and bake in moderately hot oven with increasing heat. Frosting is an improvement to this cake.

Frosting

¼ cup boiling water   White of 1 egg
1 cup granulated sugar   Flavoring

Boil sugar and water until it threads. Pour gradually on stiffly beaten egg white and beat until all has been added and frosting is of right consistency to spread. Flavor with few drops lemon-juice. If chocolate frosting is desired, melt two teaspoonfuls chocolate over hot water and stir into the white icing.

Emergency Ice-cream (to Use up Whites of Eggs)

The freezer for this receipt should hold not less than two quarts.

Make a custard with yolks of two eggs, one-fourth cup flour, two-thirds cup sugar, few grains salt, and half a can of sweetened condensed milk with water to make up a quart. When cold and ready to freeze add one cup canned evaporated milk, two tablespoonfuls vanilla, and the beaten whites of four eggs. It may be flavored with chocolate (melted over hot water and added to the hot custard), with fresh cut-up peaches rubbed through a sieve, or with bits of chopped ginger. This receipt, besides using up extra whites of eggs, is useful when fresh milk is scarce.

THE COOK BOOK OF LEFT-OVERS

Apple and Ginger Fluff (Using up Whites of Eggs)

For a half cupful of left-over whites of eggs use two-thirds of a cup sifted apple, one-fourth cup powdered sugar, few grains salt, and one teaspoonful ground or chopped crystallized ginger. Take baked apples left from breakfast, or apple sauce. Rub apple through strainer, sift sugar, put ginger through meat grinder, using finest cutter. Add salt to eggs, beat very stiff, and gradually add sugar, ginger, and a little at a time the apple, beating very hard. Pile in glass dish and put in cool place until ready to serve. It must not stand long, or it will fall. Ginger may be cut into little bits and stirred through the mixture.

Scrambled Eggs (Using up Yolks of Eggs)

Yolks of 3 eggs	1 large tablespoonful bacon cut in bits
1 whole egg	
Dash of cayenne	$\frac{1}{2}$ cup milk
Dried bread or toast	$\frac{1}{2}$ tablespoonful butter

Prepare crisp dry toast, or use oven-dried slices of bread, if at hand. Beat eggs lightly, add milk and bacon. Melt butter in hot omelet-pan, add the egg mixture, and cook lightly, holding pan up from intense heat. Have hot milk ready in saucepan, dip slices of bread or toast quickly in it, put on hot platter, and pour scrambled eggs over all.

Scrambled Matzoth—Passover Dish (Using up Yolks of Eggs)

3 small round matzoth	Yolks 3 eggs
Butter	White 1 egg
$\frac{1}{4}$ teaspoonful salt	3 tablespoonfuls of milk

EGGS

Break matzoth (a kind of cracker sold chiefly in Jewish shops) in pieces and soak in cold water until soft. Press out the water and mix with well-beaten eggs and salt. Heat pan, put in a little butter, add the matzoth mixture, and stir until eggs are lightly cooked. Serve for breakfast.

Little Gold Cakes (Using up Yolks of Eggs)

- 1 tablespoonful butter
- ½ cup sugar
- 4 egg yolks (beaten till very thick)
- ¼ cup sour cream
- ⅛ teaspoonful soda
- Scant ¾ cup sifted bread flour
- Grated nutmeg
- Few grains salt

Cream butter and sugar together, add beaten yolks, and beat hard. Combine soda, dissolved in very little hot water, with cream, add to egg mixture, quickly add flour, salt, and nutmeg, and bake in small tins. Frost when cold and place candied cherry on top of each.

MY OWN RECEIPTS

MY OWN RECEIPTS

MY OWN RECEIPTS

MY OWN RECEIPTS

MY OWN RECEIPTS

WHAT TO DO WITH LEFT-OVER FRUIT

Ripe fruit is perishable, and when the supply is within control, the housekeeper should take care to keep it limited so there will not be large quantities on hand. As soon as it shows signs of softening it is no longer fit to be served as fresh fruit, but should be cooked up at once with a little sugar added, and used as a sauce; or, with more sugar added and cooked longer, almost any fruit can be made into a good jam for future use. Only perfectly sound, fresh fruit is safe to can. Canned fruit when opened spoils more quickly than any other cooked fruit; it is therefore wise always to use any remainder as soon as possible. It can be rubbed through a sieve, a little corn-starch added for thickening, made sweeter if necessary, and cooked until it thickens, and used as a sauce for puddings. It can be molded in a corn-starch mixture, added to a muffin batter and baked, or stirred into ice-cream when the dasher is removed, or poured over ice-cream when it is served. Many other ways will suggest themselves.

Fruit Macédoine

It often happens that a little fresh fruit is allowed to spoil because there is not enough to go round again. Instead of this two or more kinds may be mixed together very acceptably. The following make good combinations: strawberries and pineapple; raspberries, currants, and a few pitted cherries; huckleberries and a few currants; peaches and pineapple; pears and peaches; orange, grape-fruit, and banana. Keep the left-overs very cold and carefully, to avoid a "mussy" appearance, and serve again promptly.

Stewed-Fruit Macédoine

A small portion of several fruits, particularly berries, may be stewed together, into an excellent sauce. The following are good combinations: cranberries and a few raisins; rhubarb and huckleberries; raspberries and currants; huckleberries and currants. Avoid long cooking of any of these, as it dissipates the flavor.

Apricot Sauce

Beat powdered sugar, apricot-juice, and pieces of fruit together. Whip white of an egg very light, and add to beaten fruit and sugar, or add fruit gradually to unbeaten egg white, and beat some minutes. Sauce made in second way will stand longer. Different fruits may be used.

Apple-Sauce Cake

1 cup light brown sugar	1 teaspoonful soda
½ cup shortening	1¾ cups bread flour
1 cup apple sauce	½ teaspoonful each mace, clove, and cinnamon
1 teaspoonful salt	

Put sugar and shortening in mixing-bowl, add apple sauce, then dry ingredients already mixed and sifted. Beat well, turn into deep pan, and bake in moderate oven about one hour. If liked, one cup of floured raisins may be added with dry ingredients. Butter alone may be used for shortening, or part chicken or rendered beef fat.

Apple Charlotte

- 1 tablespoonful gelatine
- ¼ cup sugar
- ¼ cup boiling water
- 1 tablespoonful lemon-juice
- 3 tablespoonfuls cold water
- ½ cup strained apple sauce
- 1 cup whipped cream

Soak gelatine in cold, dissolve in boiling, water. Add sugar, lemon-juice, and apple sauce (more sugar if the apple sauce is not sweet), and set in cool place to stiffen. When it is thoroughly chilled and begins to harden around the edges, beat with a Dover beater, adding gradually the whipped cream. When stiff enough to drop, pour into mold and chill. The whites of two eggs beaten stiff may be used instead of cream, and the charlotte served with soft custard.

Blackberry Jelly (with Gelatine)

- ⅔ cup blackberry-juice and pulp strained from stewed blackberries
- 1 tablespoonful lemon-juice
- ⅓ cup boiling water
- ½ tablespoonful gelatine

Soak gelatine in two tablespoonfuls cold water; when softened dissolve in boiling water; add sugar if necessary, hot blackberry-pulp, and lemon-juice. Mix, pour into bowl or mold, and set in cool place to form. Serve with sugar and cream.

Blueberry Ice

1 pint stewed blueberries (already sweetened)
½ cup sugar
⅛ cup lemon-juice
½ tablespoonful gelatine, soaked in half a cup of cold water
1 cup boiling water
1 beaten egg white

Strain berries. (Juice should amount to one and one-half cups.) Melt soaked gelatine in boiling water, add sugar, blueberry, and lemon-juice. Cool and freeze. Stir in beaten egg white just before freezing.

Stewed Cantaloup

When cantaloups are cut they are sometimes found to be too green or too tasteless to be served as fresh fruit. In such cases, cut the pulp out with a spoon or knife, add a little water, sugar according to the sweetness of the melons, and a few thin slices of lemon. Stew until tender.

Corn-starch Pudding

1 pint milk
4 tablespoonfuls corn-starch, blended in little cold water
¼ cup sugar
1 egg, well beaten
¼ teaspoonful salt
½ cup chopped cooked peaches, apricots, or pears
Flavoring

Scald milk, stir in blended corn-starch, and cook five minutes in double boiler. Place upper part

FRUIT

double boiler over fire, let corn-starch boil, return boiler to place, add sugar, egg, and salt beaten together, and cook two minutes, stirring constantly. Flavor with vanilla, add fruit, and pour into mold. Chill, and serve with sugar and cream. An excellent way of using up small amounts of canned fruits.

Fruit Cocktail

Mix one-third cup of pineapple shredded with a fork, one-half cup of sliced orange-pulp and bananas, one cup berries or grape-fruit. Pour over a dressing made of one-third cup melted currant jelly, three tablespoonfuls lemon-juice, and one-half cup of sugar. (Jelly and sugar are heated and lemon-juice added.) Chill and serve in glasses.

A Cream Filling for Cake

Take one cup of thick corn-starch custard, and mix with it one-half cup of chopped stewed prunes, drained very dry, and add a few chopped walnuts.

Emergency Salad (from Fruit and Nuts)

Cut a few bits of cheese into neat cubes. Chop six or eight olives. Break a few English walnuts in suitable-sized pieces. Remove the skin and seeds from a bunch of white grapes, if at hand. Slice a banana or orange. Cut one or two small sweet pickles in thin slivers. Mix all lightly together. Take four fair red apples. Polish them well, cut a thick slice from the stem end and take out the core and most of the apple part, so as to form a cup. Mix the salad with a little mayonnaise, and serve in the apples, replacing the slice on top.

Fruit Soufflé

¾ cup cooked and strained fruit-pulp peach, apricot, prune, or quince
Whites 3 eggs
Enough sugar to sweeten

Prepare pulp from canned or stewed fruit; add sugar if necessary; if too sweet, lemon-juice. Beat whites of eggs stiff, add gradually fruit-pulp, and beat until all has been put in. Turn into buttered molds, having them three-fourths full. Place in pan of hot water and bake in slow oven until firm. Serve with soft custard.

Soft Custard

1 pint milk
Yolks 3 eggs
Few grains salt
3 tablespoonfuls sugar
½ teaspoonful vanilla or piece lemon-rind

Scald milk with lemon-rind, beat yolks, sugar, and salt together. Combine by pouring hot milk gradually on yolks and sugar, stirring meanwhile. Strain mixture into double boiler and cook until thickened slightly. Remove at once from double boiler and cool. If vanilla is preferred, add when custard is cold.

Jelly Whip

3 tablespoonfuls any tart jelly
3 egg whites
½ teaspoonful lemon-juice
1 teaspoonful gelatine
4 tablespoonfuls rolled macaroons
A little salt

Soak the gelatine in one tablespoonful of cold water ten minutes, and then melt over hot water.

FRUIT

Add the jelly and salt to the unbeaten whites and beat stiff with a Dover beater, adding the lemon-juice and gelatine gradually. Fold in two tablespoonfuls of the macaroons and set away to chill. Put a tablespoonful of any juicy fresh or canned fruit in small glasses, pile the whip lightly on top, and sprinkle with the remainder of the macaroons.

Grape-fruit Served in Slices

One large grape-fruit can be made to serve four people at luncheon by cutting it into thick slices like a watermelon, removing the fibrous core in the center and filling the space with any fresh fruit at hand, such as strawberries, peaches, or shredded pineapple. Have all well chilled before serving.

Huckleberry Dumplings

1½ cups left-over huckleberries
4 tablespoonfuls sugar
3 tablespoonfuls water
1 teaspoonful vinegar
1 teaspoonful cinnamon

Put above ingredients into saucepan and let them come just to the boil. While these are heating sift together one cup of flour, two teaspoonfuls of baking-powder, and one-eighth teaspoonful of salt. Beat up one egg, add to it about two tablespoonfuls of milk, and stir lightly into the dry materials. There should be just liquid enough to wet the flour, and make a very stiff dough. Drop by spoonfuls into the boiling huckleberries, cover tightly, and boil ten minutes without removing the cover. Serve at once. A mixture of huckleberries and currants may be used, and the vinegar omitted.

Hasty Huckleberry Pudding

Take four slices of cut bread that has not become dry. Butter the slices on both sides. Place one each in individual sauce-dishes. Grate a very little nutmeg on the top of each, and pour over enough warm, stewed huckleberries to moisten and well cover.

Lemon Cups for Dressings

When making lemonade save the best skins by putting them at once in cold water. In this way they will keep for several days, and are nice to use in serving salad dressings with lettuce salad, or cocktail sauce with oysters or clams, or cold Hollandaise sauce with fish.

Lemon Syrup for Lemonade

Do not allow an accumulated supply of lemons to dry up or mold. They can be made into syrup which will keep for some time, and which can be used for lemonade by simply adding water. To make syrup, boil a cup of sugar with one-quarter cup of water until it threads. Add to this the juice and pulp of six lemons and the grated rind of two, being careful to grate only the thin yellow part. Let all scald together, but do not boil. Strain and bottle.

Peach Tapioca

Soak one-half cup of granulated tapioca in one and one-half cups of cold water over night. In the morning add two cups of boiling water and a little salt, and let it boil five minutes. Then put

FRUIT

into a double boiler and cook until clear. Take the remnants of a can of peaches—there should be at least a cup, and if there is a pit or two all the better. Add a little more sugar, and simmer until the syrup is somewhat thickened, and stir into the cleared tapioca. Remove from the fire, cool, and pour into a glass dish. Serve with sweetened cream.

Peach Sauce

When preserving peaches take the broken pieces and halves not perfect enough for putting in jars and make a sauce of them. Add vinegar, clove, cinnamon, and sugar, and boil all together until of the right consistency.

Peach Pudding

1 cup flour
½ cup sugar
½ cup milk
Left-over peaches, canned or fresh
2 tablespoonfuls butter
2 teaspoonfuls baking-powder
1 egg

Cream butter and sugar, add well-beaten egg, milk, and flour and baking-powder sifted together. Put a layer of peaches in a buttered baking-dish, pour the batter over, and bake. Serve with cream and sugar, or sweet sauce. Other fruits may be used instead of peaches.

Sauce of Mixed Fruit

One or two kinds of stewed fruits added to a tart stewed plum sauce will improve it and give variety. Rub the sauce through a strainer, add to it two

THE COOK BOOK OF LEFT-OVERS

or three Bartlett pears (cut fine and stewed until tender in a very little water), and a few tablespoonfuls of left-over apple sauce. Sweeten and cook together until the flavors of the fruits are well blended and the sauce has thickened slightly.

Fruit Sago (from Syrup Left from Canning)

In canning berries there is often a quantity of fruit syrup left over. Take a pint of any kind at hand, but raspberry or raspberry and currant particularly recommended, and stir into it when boiling three tablespoonfuls of sago that has been soaked in cold water several hours. Add more sugar if necessary and a little salt, and cook in a double boiler until the sago is soft. Pour in a mold and chill. This can be served with a little fresh fruit or with sweetened cream.

Fruit Whip

Put a little jelly or preserve in the bottom of lemonade glasses. Fill up with sweetened and flavored whipped cream. May be served as an evening dessert with light cakes.

Individual Shortcakes with Stewed Fruit

Measure a pint of sifted flour. Sift with it two tablespoonfuls sugar, half a teaspoonful salt, and four scant teaspoonfuls baking-powder. Cut into the mixture one-fourth cup shortening (equal parts butter and chicken fat or beef dripping may be used). Make a soft dough with about three-fourths of a cup of milk. Bake in small tins, split after baking, butter the halves and spread between and on top any left-over stewed or canned

FRUIT

fruits such as peaches, apricots, blackberries, or currants. Small amounts may be used, varying the filling if there is not enough of one kind to go around, or a meringue may be made, for the top, of the beaten whites of two eggs sweetened with three tablespoonfuls powdered sugar and flavored with lemon-juice.

Orange Peel

Do not make a practice of throwing away the skins of oranges. The grated yellow rind makes a good flavoring for cakes, candies, pudding sauces, and icings, and is much cheaper than extracts.

Candied Orange Peel

Cut the peel of three or four oranges into narrow strips and soak it twenty-four hours in enough cold water to cover, adding two tablespoonfuls of salt to each quart of water used. Pour off the salt water and rinse very thoroughly. Cover with fresh cold water and boil until almost tender. Make a syrup of two cups of sugar and one and one-quarter cups of water. When it boils add the orange peel and simmer gently until it looks clear and the syrup has thickened. Take out a few pieces at a time with a fork, roll in granulated sugar, and spread on a flat platter. Or it may be dried in the oven with the door open, packed in glass jars, and used for mince pies, puddings, etc., cut in small bits. If any syrup remains it can be used a second time, or it will flavor a pudding sauce.

Orange Baskets

When the pulp of oranges is to be served in small pieces, or the juice alone used, cut the peel in the form of baskets with a handle half an inch wide, and with a spoon carefully remove the pulp. Put the baskets at once into cold water and they will keep fresh for several days. Use them for serving orange sponge, lemon jelly, or a fruit blanc mange. An orange sponge may be attractively served to an invalid in this way. For the sponge take the juice of a medium-sized orange, strain it, add two teaspoonfuls of sugar, and stir until dissolved. Add two teaspoonfuls of cold water to one teaspoonful of granulated gelatine. When softened melt over hot water and add to the orange-juice with a few drops of lemon-juice. Set on ice until it begins to harden around the edge of the bowl, then beat with a Dover beater until the mass is thick and spongy. Chill again and pile lightly in the orange basket after it has been well dried.

Russian Tea

Add a slice of lemon and a little preserve—strawberry, raspberry, etc., to tea, served hot in glasses.

Watermelon Balls

Any watermelon left over can be attractively served as a breakfast fruit by cutting it into perfectly round balls with a vegetable scoop, or if this is not at hand, cut the pulp out with a dessert-spoon into oval-shaped pieces, chill, and serve very cold.

MY OWN RECEIPTS

MY OWN RECEIPTS

MY OWN RECEIPTS

MY OWN RECEIPTS

WHAT TO DO WITH LEFT-OVER BEVERAGES

It is always well to measure coffee and tea when preparing them for the table, so there shall be no left-overs. But there are occasions when a remainder is unavoidable. In those cases do not allow the liquid to stand on the grounds, but pour it off as soon as the meal is over. As for grape-juice, it spoils very quickly after a bottle is opened, so it should be used promptly.

Iced Coffee with Milk

Strain the coffee carefully so there are no grounds. Mix with it an equal quantity of rich sweet milk and sweeten as desired, stirring until the sugar is entirely dissolved. Let it get very cold before serving.

Coffee Jelly

½ cup good clear coffee
½ cup rich milk
½ cup boiling water
4 tablespoonfuls sugar
3 tablespoonfuls cold water
1 tablespoonful granulated gelatine
A little salt

Soak the gelatine in the cold water until softened Add the boiling water and stir until the gelatine is dissolved. Mix the coffee, milk, sugar, and salt together, and add them to the gelatine. Pour into a mold and set away to harden. Serve with whipped or plain sweetened cream and sprinkle the top with rolled macaroon-crumbs. If there is no cream, serve it with sliced bananas toned up with a little tart fruit-juice.

Clear Coffee Jelly

1½ tablespoonfuls gelatine
¼ cup cold water
½ cup boiling water
3 tablespoonfuls sugar
1 cup clear coffee
Few drops lemon-juice
Sliced bananas

Soak gelatine in cold water, melt in boiling water, add sugar, coffee, and lemon-juice When partly stiffened stir in slices of banana. Mold and serve with rich milk or whipped cream slightly sweetened.

Coffee Blanc Mange

3 cups scalded milk
1 cup strong coffee
⅓ cup sugar
5 tablespoonfuls corn-starch
1 teaspoonful butter
Salt

Blend corn-starch with some of the cold coffee, stir with remainder into scalded milk, add sugar and sprinkling of salt. Cook in double boiler five minutes, then over fire until corn-starch boils. Stir in butter just before taking up. This quantity of corn-starch, level measurement, makes a very delicate blanc mange. If preferred firmer, use six tablespoonfuls corn-starch.

BEVERAGES

Coffee Ice-cream (from Custard)

To two cups of left-over or fresh custard add one-half cup of good strong coffee and one-half cup of cream or rich milk, and sugar enough to make it quite sweet. Pour into the freezer and freeze.

Coffee Pudding (from Sponge-cake)

½ cup butter
¼ cup sugar
1 cup strong sweetened coffee, cold
8 small, stale sponge-cakes
3 yolks eggs

Cream butter and sugar, add yolks of eggs, and beat very light. Cut sponge-cake into slices and spread with creamed mixture. Pour coffee over cake, put in mold, let stand, and turn out on dish. Serve with whipped cream.

Coffee Spice Cake

½ cup butter
2 eggs
½ cup cold coffee
2 teaspoonfuls baking-powder
1 cup sugar
2 cups flour
2 teaspoonfuls mixed spices
⅛ teaspoonful salt

Cream the butter and sugar well together. Add the unbeaten eggs, one at a time, and beat the batter well. Sift together the flour, baking-powder, salt, and spices, and add them alternately with the cold coffee. Bake in a moderate oven until the cake shrinks from the side of the pan.

Tea Punch No. 1

Boil together for five minutes a quart of water, juice of three lemons, half a cup of sugar, and the shaved yellow rind of the lemons. Add a pint of cold tea (more if liked), currant, raspberry, or grape juice, pieces of shredded pineapple (canned or fresh), and sections of oranges. Add more sugar if necessary and pieces of ice. Pour in a bottle of Apollinaris or Vichy just before serving.

Tea Punch No. 2

Pour off any left-over tea from the leaves at once, and if extra strong dilute with a little boiling water run through the teapot. To a quart of such liquid add one-half cup of lemon-juice, and sugar to sweeten as desired. Stir until the sugar is entirely dissolved. Remove the rind and bitter white portion from one small orange, cut into thin slices, and each slice into quarter sections. Add this to the tea and set away to get very cold.

Cocoa Filling for Cake

Left-over cocoa can easily be made into a filling for cake by adding two tablespoonfuls of dissolved arrowroot to one cup of cocoa, reheating to the boiling-point, adding more sugar if necessary, the yolk of one egg, slightly beaten, and a little salt. Remove from the fire as soon as the egg is added. When nearly cool add one-half teaspoonful of vanilla and spread between the layers.

Cocoa and Coffee Icing

1 cup confectioner's sugar	1 teaspoonful butter
	½ teaspoonful vanilla
4 teaspoonfuls cocoa	2 tablespoonfuls of hot coffee

BEVERAGES

Reheat any cold coffee until very hot and blend it with the cocoa. Add the butter and stir in the sugar, and beat until smooth. Add the vanilla, and spread at once on a slightly warm cake.

Grape-juice Charlotte

½ cup grape-juice
2 tablespoonfuls sugar
Lemon-juice
2 teaspoonfuls granulated gelatine
White of 1 egg
A little salt
Lady-fingers

Add a teaspoonful of cold water to the gelatine and soak ten minutes. Melt over hot water, and add with the sugar to the grape-juice. Stir until the sugar dissolves. Set in a pan of cracked ice, and when it begins to harden around the edge of the bowl, beat with a Dover beater until the mass becomes thickened. Then fold into it the stiffly beaten white of one egg, to which have been added the salt, lemon-juice, and one tablespoonful of sugar while beating. Keep on ice until very cold and thick. When ready to serve, unmold in a glass dish in a border of lady-fingers.

Grape-juice Jelly

1 tablespoonful gelatine
¼ cup cold water
¼ cup sugar
1 cup grape-juice
1 tablespoonful lemon-juice
½ cup boiling water

Soak gelatine in cold water until softened, add boiling water, and stir until dissolved. Put in sugar, lemon and grape-juice, pour into bowl or mold, and set in cold place to form.

MY OWN RECEIPTS

MY OWN RECEIPTS

MY OWN RECEIPTS

MY OWN RECEIPTS

MY OWN RECEIPTS

WHAT TO DO WITH LEFT-OVER CAKE

Mock Plum Pudding (Cake)

Two cups stale cake-crumbs softened in about one-quarter cup hot milk. If crumbs are very dry it may take a little more milk. Add to the softened crumbs

1 well-beaten egg	2 teaspoonfuls mixed spices
¼ cup sugar	
¼ cup molasses (Porto Rico)	¼ teaspoonful soda
	½ teaspoonful salt
¼ cup stewed prunes, chopped	2 teaspoonfuls lemon-juice
¾ cup chopped raisins	¼ cup flour

Bake in a moderate oven forty-five minutes. Serve hot with foamy sauce.

Foamy Sauce

¼ cup butter	4 tablespoonfuls of cream or rich milk
¾ cup light-brown sugar	
A few drops lemon-juice	
	½ teaspoonful vanilla

Cream the butter, add the sugar slowly, and beat until very light. Add the cream and flavor-

THE COOK BOOK OF LEFT-OVERS

ing gradually. When ready to serve, stand the bowl over boiling water and stir until the sauce is foamy-looking.

Coffee Pudding (from Sponge-cake)

See page 215.

Trifle

Cut stale cake into slices and spread preserves between them. Lay in a deep dish and heap full of whipped cream.

Banana- and Jam-Pudding

In a buttered earthen baking-dish slice four good-sized bananas. Sprinkle them lightly with lemon-juice, and cover them with a layer of any kind of tart jam. Cream one tablespoonful of butter with four tablespoonfuls of sugar, and add the well-beaten yolks of two eggs, one cup of milk, and one cup of fine stale cake-crumbs, and a little salt. Fold in the stiffly beaten whites of the two eggs and pour the mixture over the bananas and jam. Bake in a moderate oven about half an hour. Serve at once.

Temperance Tidbits

Moisten with lemon-juice enough stale ladyfingers or thin slices of stale sponge-cake to well cover the bottom of a glass dish holding a quart. Make a soft custard by scalding two cups of milk and pouring it slowly upon two beaten egg yolks, mixed with three tablespoonfuls of sugar, one teaspoonful of butter, and a little salt. Cook in a double boiler until thickened. Strain, and when

CAKE

partly cool add one-half teaspoonful of vanilla, and pour over the cake. When ready to serve beat the whites to a stiff froth, adding one tablespoonful of sugar and a little lemon-juice while beating. Drop lightly by spoonfuls on top of the custard, and put a few bits of bright-colored jelly on the meringue.

Sponge-cake Porcupine

Cut as large squares as possible from stale sponge-cake. Place in pudding-dish, moisten with sweetened orange-juice. Blanch almonds and press into cake, sharp ends up. Prepare soft custard (see page 202) and pour over all.

Berry Whip

Fill a dish with slices of stale sponge-cake. Sugar a quart of berries, mash them slightly, and pour over cake. Beat whites of three eggs stiff, add three tablespoonfuls powdered sugar, and beat in enough berries to flavor and color. Heap on cake and serve with cream.

MY OWN RECEIPTS

MY OWN RECEIPTS

MY OWN RECEIPTS

MY OWN RECEIPTS

MY OWN RECEIPTS

DAINTY DISHES FROM LITTLE BITS

Sandwiches

It is sometimes advisable to utilize the cut slices of fresh bread that are left over by making them into sandwiches at once, and serving them the same day, rather than putting them in the breadbox and running the risk of overlooking them. Pack them in a bowl, cover with a napkin dipped in hot water and wrung out very dry, and put a plate over them. This will keep them perfectly fresh for some hours. Many little dainty bits can be used in their preparation. The following combinations will be found acceptable:

No. 1

Make a paste of cooked chicken livers with melted butter. Add lemon-juice, cayenne, salt, and chopped olives. Spread between thin slices of white bread. These sandwiches are good without the olives.

No. 2

Moisten flaked smoked whitefish with butter, add chopped sour cucumber pickles, season with mustard paste and a dash of cayenne, and use as a sandwich filling with white bread.

THE COOK BOOK OF LEFT-OVERS

No. 3
Finely minced salmon and cucumber mixed with salad dressing.

No. 4
Sardines and hard-cooked egg yolk. Remove the skin and bones from the sardines, mash them to a paste with the egg, and season with salt, pepper, and a little lemon-juice.

No. 5
Equal quantities of grated cheese and butter creamed together. Spread this on the bread and sprinkle with minced watercress.

No. 6
Finely chopped peanuts and celery mixed with salad dressing.

No. 7
Mix well together chopped nuts and raisins and a little lemon-juice. Heat through, let cool, and spread on Graham crackers. Press together lightly, and crisp in moderate oven.

A Use for Left-over Fondant
In making candy from fondant, put aside all scrapings from utensils used. These will keep indefinitely in a covered glass jar in cool, dry place, and when melted with a very little hot water, make good icing for small cakes, etc. No strong flavors, as peppermint or wintergreen, should be used.

Filling for Tarts
Take any odds and ends in the way of jelly, preserves, stewed fruit cut in small pieces, pudding

DAINTY DISHES FROM LITTLE BITS

sauces, bits of orange, cake-crumbs (dried for use as bread is dried). Combine to taste; do not have any one ingredient predominate, as there should be an indefinite flavor. Sweeten if necessary; if too sweet add lemon-juice. Cook in double boiler until it is of right consistency and looks rich. This mixture will keep two or three weeks if kept covered in a glass jar in a cool place.

For the pastry use rule for "Plain Pastry for Four Patty Pies" (see page 27), increasing the shortening to half as much again.

Jerusalem Pudding

¾ tablespoonful gelatine
¼ cup boiling water
¼ cup cold water
1 tablespoonful cooked rice (dry)
Walnuts, figs, dates, half a cup together
½ teaspoonful vanilla
½ pint heavy cream
¼ cup powdered sugar

Soak gelatine in cold water, when softened dissolve in hot water. Scald fruit, chop with nuts, and add with rice (beaten soft) to gelatine. Whip cream stiff, flavor, sweeten, and fold lightly into gelatine mixture. Place in ice-box. Serve very cold, turned out into glass dish.

Frosted Chocolate (from Left-over Ice-cream)

Add milk or cream and bits of ice to any left-over chocolate ice-cream. Serve in glasses. The custard should always be turned out from the freezer can, kept as cold as possible, and used the same day.

THE COOK BOOK OF LEFT-OVERS

Marguerites from Left-over Icing

If it happens that there is any *boiled* icing of any sort left over, set it at once in hot water so it will not harden. Cut two marshmallows in small pieces and stir them into the warm icing. Prepare a few chopped nuts and add them, together with a little shredded cocoanut. Drop by teaspoonfuls on saltines or zephyr crackers, and brown delicately in the oven.

Dates Stuffed with Left-over Icing

Add enough more confectioner's sugar to any left-over *uncooked* icing to make it quite stiff, flavor it with a little more lemon-juice or vanilla, and mix in a few chopped peanuts. Stuff the dates with this mixture.

Meringues (from Left-over Pie Crust)

Roll bits of pie crust rather thin, cut in domino shapes, prick slightly and bake. Spread thickly with any kind of jam or marmalade. Beat the white of an egg to a stiff froth, adding one tablespoonful of sugar and a little lemon-juice while beating, pile on the top, and brown lightly in the oven.

INDEX

A

Apple Charlotte, 199.
Apple and Ginger Fluff, 190.
Apple Sauce Cake, 198.
Apples, Baked (with Pork), 38.
    Fried (with Pork), 39.
Apricot Sauce, 198.
Asparagus, Soup, 103.
    Tips (with Creamed Chicken), 56.
    with Cheese, 102.
    use in Vegetable Sauce, 68.

B

BACON (AND HAM), SECTION ON, 45–48.
Bacon, and Liver Hash, 47.
    with Poached Egg (Yankee Toast), 47
    how to use fat from, 5.
Banana and Jam Pudding, 225.
Beans (Baked Beans), Rarebit, 104.
    Salad, 104.
    Soup, 103.
    and Tomato Purée, 103.
    Warmed over, 104.
BEEF, SECTION ON, 7–18.

Beef, Croquettes, 18.
    Loaf, 9.
    Pie, 9.
    Roast in Tomato Sauce, 8.
    Scallop, 18.
    Scallop of Roast with Rice, 14.
    Soufflé, 10.
    Soup, 17.
Beet, Rice and Celery Salad, 120.
Beets, Creamed, 105.
    General use in garnishing, *see* various receipts under SALADS.
Bermuda Onion and Orange Salad, 120.
Berry Whip, 225.
BEVERAGES, SECTION ON, 213–217.
Bird's-Nest Toast, 151.
Bisque, (Mock) Soup, 122.
Bisque, Oyster, 90.
Blackberry Jelly (with Gelatine), 199.
Blanc Mange, 188.
Blanket of Veal, 33.
Blueberry Ice, 200.
Bluefish, use for. See SALMON SCALLOP, 92.
Boneless "Birds," 58.
Boston Brown Bread, Receipt for, 177.
    Brewis, 151.
    in Crust Coffee, 153.
    Relish, 151.
    Toast, 151.
Boston Scalloped Fish, 84.
Braised Meat Balls, 11.
BREAD, SECTION ON, 149–160.
Bread Cereal, 153.
    Dry, and how to freshen, 150.

INDEX

Bread Griddle Cakes, 150.
    Omelet, 152.
    Pudding, 154.
    Pudding Steamed, 158.
    Pudding, to freshen, 140.
    Sauce, 153.
    Stale, general uses, 149.
    Steamed, 150.
    Sticks, 152.
Breakfast Straws, 178.
Brewis (from Boston Brown Bread), 151.
Broth, Clam, 82.
Brown Betty, 155.
Brown Sauce, 70.

C

Cabbage, Creamed in Cheese Shells, 105.
    Scallop, 105.
    Stuffed with Beef, 13.
CAKE, SECTION ON, 223–225.
Canapes, Cheese, 167.
Canapes, Salmon, 90.
Canning Syrup, use for, 206.
Cantaloup, Stewed, 200.
Caper Sauce, 70.
Caper Sauce in Old Homestead Pie, 25.
Carrot Croquettes, 106.
Carrots with Peas in Croustades, 105.
Cauliflower, Sautéd, 106.
    in Vegetable Sauce, 68.
Celery, Cooked with Chicken (Scallop), 55
    Escalloped, 107.
    Leaves, for Seasoning, 101.
    Soup, 106.

Celery, Toast, 107.
    with Peanuts in Sandwiches, No. 6, 232.
    in Vegetable Sauce, 68.
CEREAL, SECTION ON, 131–143.
Cereal, in Griddle Cakes, 132.
    Molded with Fruit, 132.
    Muffins, 143.
    with Tomato Salad, 132.
    in Tomato Salad with Fish, 124.
CHEESE, SECTION ON, 165–172.
Cheese, Canapes, 167.
    with Creamed Sprouts, 166.
    Dreams, 167.
    and Fish Soufflé, 169.
    and Green Peppers, 170.
    Macaroons, 168.
    Sandwiches (of Biscuits), 167.
    in Sandwiches, No. 5, 232.
    Sauce, 69.
    Shells with Creamed Cabbage, 169.
    Soufflé, 170.
    Soup, 170.
    Toast, 168.
Cheesed Rice, No. 1, 165.
Cheesed Rice, No. 2, 166.
Cherry Pudding, 156.
Chicken, Broth, use for, 60.
    and Cream-of-Rice Soup, 60.
    Creamed, 54.
    Creamed with Asparagus tips, 56.
    Croquettes, 55.
    Custard, 60.
    Gumbo Soup, 60.
    Hash, 57.

INDEX

Chicken, Pie, 58.
    and Rice Soufflé Scallop, 59.
    Salad, 53.
    Salad, Mock (of Pork), 39.
    Scallop with Celery, 55.
    Soufflé, 57.
    Tamale Dressing, 57.
    (or Turkey) Timbale, 54.
Chocolate Bread Pudding, 154.
Chowder, Baked, 83.
Clam Broth, 82.
Clams, with Veal, 38.
Club Sandwiches, 54.
Cocoa and Coffee Icing, 216.
Cocoa Filling for Cake, 216.
Codfish, Creamed, with Macaroni, 93.
Codfish Scallop with Rice and Eggs, 93.
Coffee, Blanc Mange, 214.
    and Cocoa Icing, 216.
    of Crusts, 153.
    Ice Cream (from Custard), 215.
    Iced, with Milk, 213.
    Jelly, 213.
    Jelly, Clear, 214.
    Spice Cake, 215.
Cold Sauces and Dressings, 72–75.
Cooked Salad Dressing, 75.
Corn, Baked, 109.
    Bread, 179.
    Cakes, 108.
    Cakes, Southern, 134.
    "Oysters," 107.
    Pudding, 109.
    Soup, 108.

Corn in Tomato Cases, 108.
Cornmeal Circles, 131.
Corn-starch Pudding, 200.
Corned Beef, Creamed, 16.
Corned Beef Hash, 16.
Corned Beef and Beet Hash, 16.
Cottage Cheese, No. 1, 179.
Cottage Cheese, No. 2, 179.
Crab Meat, Stuffed in Green Peppers, 94.
Cream Cheese, in Balls, 170.
       on Crackers, 168.
       and Green Peppers, 170.
       Salad, 167.
Cream Filling for Cake, 201.
Cream Puffs (from Pop-overs), 159.
Croquettes, Chicken, 55.
       Mutton or Lamb, 26.
       Salmon, 91.
       with Stock, 36.
Croustades, 105–106.
Croutons, 149.
Croutons, Potato, 115.
"Crust" Coffee, 153.
Cucumbers, Stewed, 110.
Currant Pudding, 155.
Custard, in Coffee Ice Cream, 215.
Custard, Soft, 202.

D

DAINTY DISHES FROM LITTLE BITS, SECTION ON, 231–234.
Dates Stuffed with Left-over Icing, 234.
Drawn Butter Sauce, 70.

INDEX

Dressings, 72–75.
Duckling Stew, 61.
Dumplings, Meat, 14.

E

Egg Sauce, 69.
EGGS, WHITES AND YOLKS, SECTION ON, 187–191.
Eggs, Cooked and left-over, general use, 187.
    Hard cooked, with Creamed Ham, 46.
    Hard cooked, with Jellied Veal, 34.
    Poached, with Bacon, 47.
    Poached and left-over, 187.
Eggless Cookies, 180.
Eggplant, Scallop of, 110.
Emergency Biscuits, 178.
Emergency Salad, 201.

F

Farina, with Baked Apples, 132.
    Pancakes, 132.
    Sponge, 132.
Filling for Tarts, 232.
Fire Island Stew, 9.
FISH, SECTION ON, 81–96.
Fish, Baked in Pepper Cases, 84.
    Balls, 87.
    Cakes, 86.
Fish, and Cheese Soufflé, 169.
    Cocktail, 82.
    Cold with Hollandaise, 82.
    Creamed, 83.
    Creamed in Potato Cups, 86.
    with Creamed Oysters, 83.

Fish, Fried, with Tomatoes (Scallop), 95.
    Hash, 94.
    Jellied, 88.
    Loaf, 85.
    Mélange, 89.
    with Mushrooms, 85.
    with Pie Crust, 94.
    Boiled, in Potato Border, 81.
    Salad, in Green Peppers, 87.
    Spiced, with White Sauce, 82.
    with Spinach Croquettes, 117.
    in Tomato Salad with Cereal, 124.
Floating Island, 187.
Foamy Sauce, 223.
Fondant, use for, 232.
French Dressing No. 1, 73.
French Dressing, No. 2, 73.
Frosting, 189.
FRUIT, SECTION ON, 197–208.
Fruit Cocktail, 201.
Fruit Macédoine, 197.
Fruit Macédoine (Stewed), 198.
Fruit Sago, 206.
Fruit Sauce (Mixed), 205.
Fruit Soufflé, 202.
Fruit Whip, 206.

G

German Pot Cheese Cake, 168.
Gingerbread (from Sour Milk), 180.
Gold Cakes, 191.
Graham Bread, receipt for, 180.
Graham Pudding, Spiced, 157.

INDEX

Grape-fruit, Spiced, 203.
Grape-juice Charlotte, 217.
Grape-juice Jelly, 217.
Green Pea Salad, 120.
Green Pea Salad in Egg Cases, 121.
Greens, Salad of, 119.

H

HAM (AND BACON), SECTION ON, 45–48.
Ham, Cakes, 47.
    Creamed, 46.
    and Eggs, Baked, 45.
    with Macaroni, 45.
    Omelet, 46.
    Sandwich Filling, 47.
Hard Sauce, 158.
Hash, Chicken, 57.
    Corned Beef, 16.
    Corned Beef and Beet, 16.
    Liver and Bacon, 47.
Hollandaise Sauce, 72.
Hominy, Balls, 133.
    with Bacon, 134.
    and Cheese Soufflé, 133.
    Fried, in Sardine Relish, 96.
    Griddle Cakes, 134; *See also* WHEATENA GRIDDLE CAKES, 143.
    Pudding, 134.
Horseradish Sauce, 7.
Hotel Club Sandwiches, 54.
Huckleberry Dumplings, 203.
Huckleberry Pudding, 204.

I

Ice-Cream (Chocolate), if left-over, *see* FROSTED
    CHOCOLATE, 233.
Ice-Cream (Coffee), receipt for, 215.
Ice-Cream, Emergency, 189.
Icing, use if left-over. *See* MARGUERITES, 234,
    and Stuffed Dates, 234.
Indian Pudding (Mock), 155.
Irish Potato Cake, 116.
Irish Rissoles, 14.

J

Jellied Fish, 88.
Jellied Tomato Salad, 123.
Jellied Veal, 34.
Jelly Whip, 202.
Jerusalem Pudding, 233.

K

Kedjeree, 89.
Kidney Bean Salad, 119.
Kitchen bouquet, use in sauces, see *Note*, 71.

L

Lady-fingers. *See* CAKE SECTION, 223–225.
LAMB (AND MUTTON), SECTION ON, 23–28.
Lamb, in Ambush, 24.
    Chartreuse (in Ambush). *See* above.
    Scallop, 26.
    Turkish Style, 23.
Lamb's Liver Hash, 27.
Lemon Cups for Dressing, 204.
Lemon Sauce, No. 1, 142.

INDEX

Lemon Sauce, No. 2, 155.
Lemon Syrup for Lemonade, 204.
Lettuce (Cream of) Soup, 110.
Level Measurements, 4.
Lima Bean Soup, 112.
Lincoln Pudding (Rice), 141.
Liver and Bacon Hash, 47.
Liver, Minced, 47.
Lobster, see CROQUETTES WITH STOCK, 36.

M

Macaroni, Baked, 111.
    in Cheese Shells, 111.
    in Fire Island Stew, 9.
    with Ham, 45.
    Savory, 111.
    with Smoked Beef, 111.
    in Tomato Cases, 111.
Macédoine Fruit, see FRUIT MACEDOINE, 197.
Macédoine Garnish, 101.
Maître d'Hôtel Butter, 74.
Maple Sauce, 158.
Marrow, deviled, on Crackers, 17.
Matzoth, 190.
Mayonnaise Dressing, 74.
Mélange, Fish, 89.
Meringue (from Pie Crust), 234.
MEATS, SECTION ON, 5–48.
Measurements, 4.
Meat Dumplings, 14.
Milk Toast, 152.
Minced Beef, Potato Border, 13.
Minced Liver, 47.

Mixed Salad (Italian), 119.
Mock Bisque Sauce with Cheese, 71.
Mock Bisque Soup, 122.
Mock Chicken Salad, 39.
Mock Lobster, 84.
Mock Plum Pudding, 223.
Mushroom Sauce, 69.
Mushroom Sauce (with Chicken Timbale)
Mushrooms. *See* VEGETABLE SAUCE, 68.
Mustard Sauce, 75.
MUTTON (AND LAMB), SECTION ON, 23–28

N

New England Pan Pie, 157.
Nuts with Raisins in Sandwiches, No. 7

O

Oatmeal Bread, 135.
    Browned, 135.
    Gruel, 135.
    Molded with Raisins, 135.
Old Homestead Pie, 25.
Olive Sauce, 71.
Olive Sauce (with Sliced Lamb), 23.
Omelet, Bread, 152.
    Ham, 46.
    with Vegetables, 102.
Onion and Potato Scallop, 112.
Orange and Bermuda Onion Salad, 120.
Orange Baskets, 207.
Orange Peel, 207.
Orange Peel Candied, 207.
Oriental Stew, 24

INDEX

Oyster Bisque, 90.
Oysters, with Panned Lamb, 28.
Oysters, with Veal Scallop, 34.
"Oysters" (Corn), 107.

P

"Pandowdy," 157.
Panned Lamb (with Oysters), 28.
Parsley Leaves, for Seasoning, 101.
Parsnip Cakes, 112.
Passover dish (Matzoth), 190.
Pastry for Patty Pies, 27.
Pea Salad, 120.
Pea Salad in Egg Cases, 121.
Pea Soup, 112.
Peas, use in Vegetable Sauce, 68.
Peach Pudding, 205.
Peach Sauce, 205.
Peach Tapioca, 204.
Peppers, Stuffed, with Beef, 12.
Peppers, Stuffed, with Crab Meat, 94.
Pie, Beef, 9.
    Chicken, 58.
    Old Homestead (Mutton), 25.
Pies, Patty Pan, 27.
Pie Crust (left-over), for Cheese Sticks, 169
                        for Meringues, 234.
Pilau, 24.
Pop-overs (for Cream Puffs), 159.
PORK (AND VEAL), SECTION ON, 33–40.
Pork, with Fried Apples, 39.
    (fresh), with Baked Apples, 38.
    Roast, and Cabbage Scallop, 39.

Pork, for Chicken Salad, 39.
    Savory Fresh, 38.
Pot Cheese Cake, 168.
Pot Roast Pie, 10.
Potato, Baked, and Cheese Scallop, 113.
    Balls, 115.
    with Cheese, 116.
    Chopped, 112.
    Creamed, 115.
    Croutons, 115.
    Cups, 86.
    and Onion Scallop, 112
    Patties, 114.
    Pyramids, 114.
    Salad, 113.
    Salad, Hot, 120.
    Soup, Cream of, 114.
    Soup, with Turnips, Cream of, 125.
    Stewed, 113.
Potato Flour, where to buy, 3; use for, 67.
Poulette Sauce, 69.
POULTRY, SECTION ON, 53–61.
Purée of Vegetable, 102.

R

Raisin Sauce, 159.
Rarebit, Baked Bean, 104.
    Tomato, 166.
    Welsh, 171.
    Welsh (Mock), 171.
Rice, with Apples, 136.
    with Roast Beef Scallop, 14.
    Beet and Celery Salad, 120.

INDEX

Rice, Cheesed, No. 1, 165.
      Cheesed, No. 2, 166.
      in Cheese Shells, 137.
      Croquettes, Sweet, 142.
      in Griddle Cakes, 141.
      Custard, No. 1, 139.
      Custard, No. 2, 140.
      Muffins, 138.
      Omelet, 137.
      Pudding, Baked, 140.
      Pudding (with Corn Starch), 141.
      Pudding, German, 139.
      Pudding (Lincoln), 141.
      Pudding, how to freshen, 140.
      and Sausage Cakes, 48.
      Soup, with Vegetables, 138.
      Soup, Cream of Rice and Chicken, 60.
      with Tomatoes, No. 1, 137.
      with Tomatoes, No. 2, 137.
Risotto, 139.
Rissoles, Irish, 14.
Russian Tea, 208.

S

SALAD.—FOR ALL VEGETABLE SALADS, *see* page 118–122.
Salad, Chicken, 53.
      Chicken, Mock (Pork), 39.
      Cream Cheese, 167.
      Emergency (Fruit and Nut), 201.
      Fish, in Green Peppers, 87.
      Fish and Potato, 89.
      Potato, 113.

Salad, Potato, Hot, 120.
    Salmon, 92.
    Shad Roe, 87.
Salmon, Canapés, 90.
    Croquettes, 91.
    with Cucumbers for Sandwiches, No. 232.
    Loaf, 92.
    Salad, 92.
    Scallop, 92.
    Smoked, 93.
    Soup, 91.
Sandwiches, Club, 54.
    Roast Beef, Hot, 8.
    See also group on pages 231–232.
    Ham Filling for, 47.
Sardines, Broiled on Toast, 95.
    Relish, 96.
    Sandwiches, with Hard-cooked Eggs, 232
    Sandwiches, Toasted, 96.
    with Tomato Catsup, 95.
SAUCES, SECTION ON, 67–75.
Sausage and Rice Cakes, 48.
Savory Meat, 18.
Savory Tomato Sauce, 71.
Scrambled Eggs, 190.
Shad Roe Salad, 87.
Shepherd's Pie, 15.
Shortcakes (individual), with Stewed Fruit, 206
Snow Pudding, 188.
Soft Custard, 202.
Soup Meat, in Beef Croquettes, 18.
    in Savory Meat, 18.
SOUR MILK AND CREAM, SECTION ON, 177–181.

INDEX

Sour Cream Dressing, 75.
Sour Cream Filling for Cake, 181.
Sour Milk Griddle Cakes, 178.
Sour Milk Gingerbread, 180.
Spanish Stew, 25.
Spice Cake, 181.
Spinach, with Baked Eggs, 118.
    Creamed in Carrot Cups, 117.
    Croquettes (with Fish), 117.
    Salad, 121.
Sponge Cake, for Coffee Pudding, 224.
Sponge Cake Porcupine, 225.
Sprouts, Creamed, with Cheese, 166.
Squash Pudding, 118.
Stale Bread, general use, 149; also Section BREAD throughout.
Stock, use of, 67.
Succotash, 104.
Supplies, general, 3.
Surprise Biscuits, 12.
Sweet Potatoes, Browned, 117.
       Croquettes, 117.
Syrup from canning, use for, 206.

T

Tamale Dressing (Chicken), 57.
Tartare (Sauce), 74.
Tea Punch No. 1, 215.
Tea Punch No. 2, 216.
Tea, Russian, 208.
Temperance Tidbits, 224.
Toast, Bird's-Nest, 151.
    Milk, 152.

Toast, Soft Buttered, 152.
    Pudding, 158.
    Tomato, 124.
    Tomato and Cheese, 125.
Trimmings (Meat). *See* page 5, on INTEL
    BUYING OF MEAT; *also* BRAISED
    BALLS, 11.
Trifle, 224.
Turkey, Timbale, 54; *also* chicken receipts
Turnip and Potato Soup, Cream of, 125.
Tomato, Cases (with Corn), 108.
    Paste, 124.
    Paste, where to buy, 3.
    Rarebit, 166.
    Salad, Jellied, 123.
    Salad (with Cereal and Fish), 124.
    Sauce (Savory), 71.
    Sautéd with Sauce, 122.
    Scalloped, 123.
    with Scrambled Eggs, 123.
    Toast, 124.
    Toast, Tomato and Cheese, 125.
Twentieth Century Hash, 12.

U

Utensils, 3.

V

Vanilla Sauce, 156.
VEAL (AND PORK), SECTION ON, 33-40.
Veal, in Batter, 35.
    Blanket of, 33.

INDEX

Veal, with Clams, 38.
      Creamed, on Biscuits, 35.
      Croquettes, with Stock, 36.
      Jellied, 34.
      Loaf, 37.
      and Potato Puff, 35.
      Rolls, 36.
      and Sago Soup, 37.
      Scallop, 38.
      Scallop with Oysters, 34.
      on Toast, 37.
Victoria Meat, 59.
Veau à la Blanquette (Blanket of Veal), 33.
VEGETABLES, SECTION ON, 101–125.
Vegetable Hash, 102.
Vegetable Salads, 118–122.
Vegetable Sauce, 68.
Vegetarian Loaf, 159.

W

Watermelon Balls, 208.
Welsh Rarebit, 171.
Welsh Rarebit (Mock), 171.
Wheatena Griddle Cakes, 143.
White Cake, 188.
White Sauce No. 1, 67.
              No. 1, A, 68.
              No. 2, 68.
              No. 3, 68.
              No. 4, 68.
WHITES (AND YOLKS) OF EGGS, SECTION ON, 191.
Winter Salad, 121.

THE COOK BOOK OF LEFT-OVERS

Y

Yankee Toast, 47.
YOLKS (AND WHITES) OF EGGS, SECTION ON, 187-191.

THE END

www.ingramcontent.com/pod-product-compliance
Lightning Source LLC
Chambersburg PA
CBHW011954150426
43199CB00019B/2863